The Double-Blind Ghost Box

The Double-Blind Ghost Box

Scientific Methods, Examples, and Transcripts

Shawn Taylor & Daniel Morgan

iUniverse, Inc.
Bloomington

THE DOUBLE-BLIND GHOST BOX
SCIENTIFIC METHODS, EXAMPLES, AND TRANSCRIPTS

iUniverse books may be ordered through booksellers or by contacting:

iUniverse
1663 Liberty Drive
Bloomington, IN 47403
www.iuniverse.com
1-800-Authors (1-800-288-4677)

ISBN: 978-1-4759-8529-0 (sc)
ISBN: 978-1-4759-8531-3 (hc)
ISBN: 978-1-4759-8530-6 (e)

Library of Congress Control Number: 2013906570

Printed in the United States of America

iUniverse rev. date: 4/22/2013

Endorsement

"... a book that should be a part of any serious
paranormal investigator's library."

Shawn and Dan have dedicated their investigative and research
talents to refining what I believe will be one of the most-used
techniques and tools in every haunting investigation, the Double-
and Triple Blind Ghost Box process. They have produced a book
that should be a part of any serious paranormal investigator's
library. Now you do not have to be a sensitive or medium to
communicate with the dead; you can hear their answers while
carrying out the investigation and be able to validate what your
team's sensitive is telling you. Having worked with Shawn, Dan,
and their team at SAI at Antietam and Gettysburg battlefields, I
know firsthand the integrity of their mission: to prove that there
is life after death. This book is a must-read!

—Patrick K. Burke
Author and battlefield/historical haunting expert

Table of Contents

Chapter Seven

Chapter Eight

Chapter Nine

Acknowledgments

We would like to extend a special thanks to the following for their ideas and support for the publication of this book. Without you it could not have happened.

Amanda Nixon, Amy Buchanan, Beverly Boehm,
Billy Meadows, Brandon Buchanan, Brenda Barton,
Bryan Payne, David Henderson, Kiesi Morgan,
Kim Payne, Malachi Taylor, Mary Russell
Michael Morgan, Patrick Burke, Shelly Taylor, Tim Oliver,
The Ramsey Middle School, Bluefield, West Virginia
The American Battlefield Ghost Hunters Society
The Col. James Graham House, Lowell, West Virginia
The Giles County Historic Society, Virginia
The Mountain Lake Hotel and Resort, Virginia
The Pearis Theatre, Narrows, Virginia
YouTube "Supernatural Media" Subscribers
and John

The Supernatural Anomaly Investigations (SAI) Team

About the Authors

Shawn Taylor, cofounder of Supernatural Anomaly Investigations (SAI), was born in Hampton Roads, Virginia, and has a long history with the supernatural. As a youth he had several run-ins with ghosts, demons, and angels—not to mention all the many unexplained phenomena that birthed his interest in the field of paranormal investigations. He began studies across a wide variety of spiritual belief systems. His pursuit for knowledge stretched him to examine diverse doctrines as well as those considered commonplace. These included, but were not limited to, Buddhism, Wicca, Necromancy, the book of Kabbalah, and the Bible. Finally, in 1992, Shawn had a near-death experience, which changed his life forever. It opened his eyes to the reality of the afterlife and the relative nature of time, space, and matter in existence. This single event sealed the deal on his soul for Christ as his personal savior. Today he hunts after the supernatural to bring to light the truth that seems to have eluded science until now. With the SAI team Shawn brings to the table a firsthand account of the afterlife. However, in this life, he brings a technical background in computer hardware, software, programming, digital media, Six Sigma problem solving, statistical analysis, psychology, counseling, and, finally, an insight for innovation. Don't be fooled: it takes a lot to spook this guy. He won't easily believe something is "paranormal" without first exhausting himself for a logical explanation. It is this insatiable need for answers that presses him to continue his explorations to this day.

Dan Morgan, cofounder of SAI, was born in Galax, Virginia, and began his experiences with the supernatural at an early age. Dan's interest in the paranormal stems from those experiences and an intense curiosity as to the science of all things supernatural. Dan sought for years for an answer to the origin of the supernatural; in 1992 he accepted Christ and began to focus his search through his experience as a Christian. For years Dan has studied science, concentrating his studies on quantum physics. After seeing similarities between quantum phenomena and the supernatural, he realized that there may be ways to study one through the other. He wishes not only to better understand the phenomena, but also to further research the field. Dan has degrees in behavioral science and electrical engineering, which he hopes to utilize to build better equipment for detection of the paranormal.

Together, Shawn and Dan, with a team of investigators, strive to uncover the mysteries of the supernatural using scientific methodology. With training in process design and electrical engineering, together they developed the Double and Triple Blind Ghost Box methods fully disclosed in this book.

Preface

"Fringe science is a study of theories that departs from the mainstream. It is remarkable that many widely accepted concepts were once considered fringe or even impossible such as atoms, airplanes, space travel, continental drift and the big bang." *Dr. Michio Kaku*

Since the dawn of time, man has explored beyond the reaches of his understanding. That which is not known to us beckons to come and see … if we dare. Many turned their backs; some covered their faces and peeked between their fingers with fear; while others watched from a distance as brave sailors set sail on an unknown sea. They waited to see if the adventurous would fall over the edge of the known world into the abyss or discover a whole new country. Nevertheless, the captains pressed on against the odds, personal fears, and public criticisms, and found an entirely new world. Many scientific breakthroughs have come from people who were considered heretics or lunatics. It is because of their perseverance that we have much of the knowledge that we do today.

Paranormal research is by no means new. It is a difficult field of study because it seems to defy all explanation and remain just out of our reach. Scientists rely on repeatable and reproducible controlled experiments, and paranormal events are by their very definition non-normal events. However, the paranormal is, ironically, one of the only frontiers that we race toward because of our own mortality, which is a certainty. At some point everyone ponders the questions and hypotheses about what happens after death. Even those who never admit to having a paranormal or supernatural experience will meet them head-on in death—unless, of course, we cease to exist once we die. So the paranormal holds a fascination for even the toughest skeptic. It is that fascination that continues to compel researchers to find that hidden treasure: proof of the supernatural.

In recent years the paranormal has gained new footing as "reality TV" has grabbed onto this research and created a cultural frenzy concerning it. People watch from the relative safety of their homes as researchers creep into dark houses and crypts, desperately looking for evidence of the afterlife. All the while these spectators ponder the "truth" behind the boisterous claims. Yet, in the back of their minds they can always rely on the thought: "This stuff could all be fake. I mean, it is just TV, after all, right?" On the other hand, for those who have done the research and have crawled into the dark holes and alleys of the human experience, the truth becomes all too apparent. The evidence of the paranormal exists for those who are willing to believe that the paranormal exists.

In fact, if you ask most researchers why they do what they do, they will most likely tell you about some paranormal experience that they had and their desire to find out what was behind it. Some groups exists only to debunk and not to prove. That is okay, as long as you are able to keep an open mind once all explanations are exhausted. Granted, there comes a level of faith with all paranormal research, because in this age digital manipulation is possible from any computer, and there are a few of them out there. But just because one *can* reproduce a paranormal event through trickery or manipulations does not mean that the event was fiction to begin with. For example, most if not all EVP (Electronic Voice Phenomena) can be explained by someone simply whispering into a microphone; but that doesn't make all EVP invalid.

As with all research and discoveries, there are always skeptics. They play a very important role in this research, because without them, there would be no balance. Skeptics help keep the trade honest. In fact, many teams include a skeptic among them, helping to balance out the ghost-under-every-rock mentality. When it comes to skepticism concerning this book, we have no problem. To be honest, when we first began using a ghost box, we too were very skeptical. As you read through this book, you will learn the process by which we began to research this tool and determined its usefulness in researching the paranormal. But, hopefully, you will come to the same conclusion we did: there is something to the ghost box when used correctly.

—Shawn Taylor and Dan Morgan

Chapter One

From Skeptics to Believers

What is a ghost box?

"What is a ghost box?" you may ask. A ghost box is basically an electronic device that sweeps a wide band of frequencies without stopping. These bands can and usually do include the frequencies of your standard AM/FM radio. Many of these devices are, in fact, converted radios. The device scans through the different frequencies at varying rates while the Listeners try to hear a message from the great beyond.

High standards for paranormal investigations

When we began our research about the ghost box, we decided from the start that no matter the outcome, we would be as transparent as possible. Our goal was to allow any and all to take our findings and come to their own conclusions. Our paranormal investigations adhere to strict scientific guidelines for all our team members. When processing evidence we look for all possible natural explanations for the event being observed. With that being said, we understand that this level of scrutiny is not for everyone. Nevertheless, we believe that it is necessary to practice the scientific method[1] when conducting investigations. Ironically, our findings have been so spectacular that when people see the evidence, it seems unbelievable. We have been accused on more than one occasion of fabricating our results. Oddly enough, it is these critics that give us the most pleasure. While this obviously does not help to convince others that our findings are valid, it does prove to us that we are not "just hearing things." When a critic hears the same thing we do and the only support for his or her lack of belief is that we fabricated evidence, it validates our findings, because we know we did not.

Ghost box experiments are remarkable

If you have never seen our videos,[2] it is hard to understand just how incredible the process is to watch. While we were conducting a battlefield investigation in Gettysburg, a couple who was visiting the site happened upon us during a ghost box experiment. The Listener with the box in this case was Shawn. He had his hood up and head down while Patrick, the Questioner, asked specific questions about battle events. The couple listened as Shawn provided responses from the ghost box to Patrick's questions. The responses were coming so quickly and were following the questions so closely that one of them said, "He must be a psychic." They were even more amazed when Shawn removed his hood to reveal that he had on headphones and could not hear any of the questions Patrick had asked! This is at the very heart of the double-blind process, and it is sessions like this where the ghost box really shines.

Patrick Burke (Questioner) and Shawn Taylor (Listener)
Double Blind Ghost Box Experiment / Triangle Field, Gettysburg

The beginning

We would like to take you through the process by which we eventually accepted the ghost box as a valid tool for paranormal investigations. Keep in mind that we did not start this process lightly. We encourage anyone who wishes to follow this path to take the same approach. We took a long time to include the ghost box in our evidence. When we began our double-blind experiments, we wanted to make sure that what we were hearing was truly supernatural. Any researcher should take an objective approach to his or her investigations. The ghost box takes time to get used to, and you may or may not have good results right away. No matter how you begin, you should use this method in a way that can validate findings and verify that what you're hearing is truly supernatural. The bottom line is that a ghost box should be one tool, but not the only tool, at your disposal.

Variation of responses by location

As we continued the research in a variety of venues, we were shocked time and time again not only at our findings, but at how differently each location responded from the ghost box. Some locations gave no coherent responses whatsoever. We have been on investigations where the box never produced a valid response. We have been on investigations where the box would talk so much we could not keep up. We perform investigations in both daylight and darkness, and there seems to be no difference in how the box performs. Through the cases we present, you will see this diversity of responses and "moods." We do not believe that this is the box's fault, but instead that it speaks of the disposition of the entities present at each location.

Variation in the number of spirits

We have investigated a few cemeteries, which have exhibited their own unique dispositions. Here, as one may expect, the ghost box was crowded with people that wanted to communicate. Some spirits are open to speak and others are not. The problem with cemeteries is that the experience can be so overwhelming that you may not be able to distinguish who is talking and who is answering. We have had incredible experiences at them, though, and in this book we will share with you one of the most incredible.

Variation between users

We have also used two different ghost boxes in tandem with two separate Listeners to see what would happen. The results were astounding! When two Listeners utilized the double blind on two separate boxes, what began to happen was a sort of dual answer. However, this is not what we expected. Obviously, we knew that it was impossible that both radios would browse the frequencies at the same time. Different radios have different speeds at which they sweep through frequencies, thus making any kind of synchronization impossible. The boxes also began finishing each other's sentences. At one point, we almost felt like we were watching a tennis match between the two Listeners. This is to say that one box would start talking to the second box and the second would answer back!

Variation between boxes

So we began the experiment. What happened was that when we would ask a question, we would get an answer from both boxes using different words! One box would say "yes" while the other would say "affirmative." At one point, the boxes seemed to begin talking to each other. A casual observer would see two people talking to each other, not realizing that they couldn't hear the responses. It was a really strange occurrence.

Variation between tools

The first case that began to focus us on the ghost box was an investigation at Ramsey Middle School in Bluefield, West Virginia. The first time we arrived at this location, we used the ghost box near the end of the night and began getting signals from an entity. We were employing a technique by which an electromagnetic field (EMF) detector was used to give a yes/no response by blinking once or twice respectively. We have used this method in the past, with its obvious limitations. When we began to use the ghost box, we used the EMF detector to determine if the devices agreed with each other. We began to shape our questions to the answers we were receiving on the box, with incredible results. The first double-blind experiment was a success.

Ghost box hide-and-seek tests

We returned to this location for a second time and truly had our minds blown. The school has five floors, providing quite the workout, especially when dragging up equipment. We were on the third floor and were fishing for answers with the box. As we began the session, we were shocked when the rhythmic pulsing of stations seemed to quiet and a voice began to "instruct us" as to what we needed to do. We later would understand this to be an entity known as John. We discuss this more in later chapters. After this brief session, a spirit began to tell us about letters that she wanted to find. We began to ask the entity, whom we believed to be a girl named Edith, where these letters could be found. She stated on the ghost box that they were in a safe in the basement, so we made our way there.

When we got there, we began to ask where the safe might be. The entity began to talk about a brown box, but we were having a hard time determining exactly where the box was. There were three members participating in this exercise, so we decided to fan out in a triangle to see if we could determine in which direction the safe was. We used this method and determined the direction in which the box lay, but we still could not pinpoint its location. The entity then instructed us to start at the fireplace and walk forty-five feet. Since we knew the direction, we began to pace off the distance. As Dan finished up at the end of the measurement, he looked down, and there was an old, rusted electrical box, lying partially covered in a sand pile. As he picked it up, the ghost box declared: "You got it!" Obviously, there were no letters in the box, but this incident revealed that the ghost box was able to lead us to the brown box.

When we revealed our findings to the owner, he indicated that the "closet like structure" about five feet away, in the center of that room, was the old safe for the school board records!

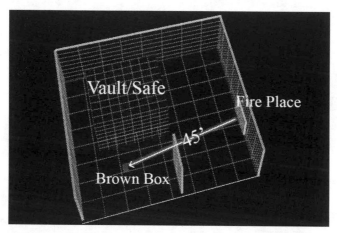

The little brown box in the basement at Ramsey Middle School

The "F" test

On another occasion we were investigating the property of one of our own members, Dave Henderson. His family had owned this property for generations, and he was curious to see what we would find if we investigated. One of the things that he wanted to focus on was an old family burial site that had been lost over the years. He had heard stories of the cemetery but had been unable to locate it on his hundreds of acres. We began the ghost box session and inquired as to the location of the gravesite. The box began to lead us in a particular direction, so we followed. As we continued it became clear that the box was focused on an area that was overgrown with briars. A detail that Dave had learned from his family was that there was a stone marked with an "F" carved into its top. As we kept searching for grave markers and coming up empty, one of the team members found the stone and observed the "F" carved there. We were unable to find the grave markers, but the stone was exactly where the ghost box said the site was.

Amanda Nixon points out the "F" stone grave marker

It is details like this that make the ghost box an incredible tool. When you are able to pinpoint details of the history, it not only helps you to find out historical details, but also determines with whom you speak. In other words, if you receive details concerning the Civil War then the entity you are speaking with may come from that period of time and be easier to identify. Details like this can be used to prove the validity of the ghost box and prove to the critics that there is more to it than just a jumble of radio stations. In the case of the ghost box, although Dave knew which direction the site was in, he had no definite details. The fact that it was dark during the session makes it that much more incredible. Even more incredible was that when we thought we were cold about the location and wandered away from that site, the box would tell us to go back. This helps to substantiate that the box was guiding us, and not the other way around. At this point we hope you see a clear potential application for the ghost box to assist in even non-paranormal cases like finding a missing person, which is an upcoming experiment for our team.

Variation in types of spirit

During that same investigation, we began a ghost box session in the same room where the box was found. Then a peculiar thing happened. A voice began to come across very clearly, introducing itself as John. It explained that we needed to keep doing what we are doing, that we could make a difference. This single experience began to shape what our group does today. One of the questions we get asked a lot is "Who is John?" Our answer: "We don't know." To be honest, when John shows up during our investigation, he is very task-focused and rarely, if ever, speaks with us directly. We have never tried to ask questions, because he doesn't appear to want to answer any. The philosophy of who or what John is goes beyond the scope of this book. We just want to point out that there are entities that may manipulate the box in greater ways than we are used to, so be prepared. Demonic or nonhuman spirits appear to have a greater control as well, and we have encountered a few throughout our investigations.

The next time that John showed up in an investigation was at Pearis Cemetery in Pearisburg, Virginia. When we arrived, we performed our investigation in our normal manner, receiving some interesting EVP but little else. At the end of the night, we began our ghost box session. Often we will try to have one group session with the entire team in attendance. This night there were only four of us present, so we all sat around and began our attempt to establish communication. Immediately a chorus of voices began to flood in, asking for help. We began to speak with these voices and got a picture of what was happening just beyond our ability to perceive. Basically, the voices kept repeating the phrase "ten thousand years, ten thousand years." This intrigued us, because we knew that the radio would not be repeating this in a normal radio scan. It was so incredible that at one point the Listener had others listen, and it was obvious to all that it was repeating this phrase. As we began to point our questions in this direction, we learned that these spirits had been told that if they would only wait ten thousand years, redemption would come. When we began to ask who had said this, they referred to a demon. We began to speak with these spirits, telling them that they had been lied to, when the demon spoke up and began telling us to leave. When we refused and began telling *it* to leave, a funny thing happened. As we were speaking to this thing, the night, which was completely still, began to stir and a fairly bad wind began to blow. At one point, the ghost box said *"Walk!"* very clearly. Five seconds later we heard a voice snarl from the corner of the cemetery, *"Walk!"* Of course the Listener never heard this. Eventually, the "strong man" was dealt with, and we were able to help the spirits. This entire scene is available on our website.

Ghost box validates history

The final case, and perhaps the most bizarre one to date, is a battlefield investigation we conducted with Patrick Burke, a founder of the American Battlefield Ghost Hunters Society. In this session we made contact pretty quickly. The details of the battle were mind-boggling. We were given details that we had no prior knowledge of as well as of what units were present. All of this was later substantiated through historical accounts. At one point Patrick asked if they had to charge back in to retrieve their dead commander. When he asked a second time, a voice replied, "Isaac? He's dead over there." The name of the commander in question was Colonel Isaac Nicoll.[3] We were flabbergasted at the level of detail. What made this session so bizarre was that during most of the session, the sounds of guns and cannons could be heard in the background. Shawn stated that he felt like he was there in the midst of the battle. At one point, a cannon with a very distinct sound could be heard. It was clear enough in the recording that, after research, it could be traced back to a twelve-pound howitzer.

This session was also unique in that we had tried a new training technique that also helped to establish our triple-blind ghost box session. In this a splitter was introduced, allowing a second Listener to be included to validate what was heard. This was important in this case, because at one point both Listeners could hear "angelic music" cutting through the radio chatter very clearly. It was so clear and distinct that they were both very excited during this time frame. However, when the recording was played back, no music could be heard. Why? We aren't sure. To be honest, we had not encountered this phenomenon before and did not know what to make of it. Outside of philosophical explanations, it's possible the recorder couldn't pick up the frequencies, although we find this to be a bit hard to swallow. No matter what the reason, the music was heard and substantiated through a second Listener but was not recorded.

Variation in languages and dialects

Just as you would expect when traveling to different areas, we run into a variety of different spirits who wish to communicate. We have heard different languages, including what has sounded French and Native American. This obviously presents new challenges to the Listener but also lends credence to the device. We have been to locations in which it appears that the spirits have very little energy, in that you can hear them but they are faint and easily lost in the noise and static that is inherent in the device. As you use the device in your own investigations, it is important that you be open and listen for the subtleties. If you are the Listener, just say whatever you hear, because it rarely makes sense to you, as you do not hear both sides of the conversation. Many times on our investigations, the Listener stops and asks if it is making any sense. These are usually some of the more incredible conversations.

Chapter Two

The History of the Ghost Box and How to Get One

About EVP: Electronic Voice Phenomenon

Perhaps one of the most controversial tools in the paranormal researcher's bag is the ghost box. Before you can understand the theory behind the ghost box, you must first understand a little about Electronic Voice Phenomenon (EVP). In this process (which was discovered in the late 1950s by Attila von Szalay[1]), a researcher receives an audible message on a voice recorder. These messages are not detected by the researcher's ears, but only on the device itself. The problem with this method is that messages can be received only after the researcher replays the device. This means that no real two-way communication can be achieved using this method in real time. If you are familiar with TV shows like *Ghost Hunters*, *Ghost Adventures*, *Paranormal State*, and *Ghost Lab*, to name a few, EVP are typically seen during evidence review. The team would play an audio file made with a recorder either placed in a room or on an investigator during the time of the investigation. Within the audio file an "unknown voice" would be heard and the team would display on the screen what they believed were the words or phrases stated. Again, this is all after the fact. Suppose the EVP caught was of significant importance, even leading to the possibility of bringing the case to closure. EVP rip away the team's opportunity to respond to the spirit who produced the EVP in the first place. So that is where the ghost box comes in. Granted, most recent advancements in recorder technology have allowed devices to record, then play back, almost instantly revealing EVP on the fly. These devices are called recorders with "EVP Live Listening Capability" and are becoming more and more popular.

The Prehistory

Incidentally, in the 1920s Thomas Edison was believed to have created a device to conduct two-way communications with those who had passed. In an article for the *Scientific American* October 30th 1920, he stated, "I have been thinking for some time of a machine or apparatus which could be operated by personalities which have passed on to another existence or sphere... I do claim that it is possible to construct an apparatus which will be so delicate that if there are personalities in another existence or sphere who wish to get in touch with us in this existence or sphere, this apparatus will at least give them a better opportunity to express themselves than the tilting tables and raps and Ouija boards and mediums and the other crude methods now purposed to be the only means of communication... I believe that if we are to make any real progress in psychic investigation, we must do it with scientific apparatus and in a scientific manner, just as we do in medicine, electricity, chemistry, and other fields...Now what I purpose to do is to furnish psychic investigators with an apparatus which will give a scientific aspect to their work...I have been working out the details for some time; indeed, a collaborator in this work died only the other day... I am not promising communication with those who have passed out of this life. I merely state that I am giving the psychic investigators an apparatus which may help them in their work, just as optical experts have given the microscope to the medical world. And if this apparatus fails to reveal anything of exceptional interest, I am afraid that I shave have lost faith in the survival of personality as we know it in this existence."[2]

Although this device was never recovered,[3] thus plunging it into the realm of Edison mythology, the article does bring to light his genuine interest in the topic.

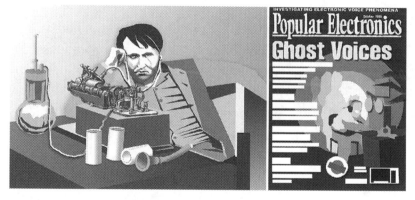

Thomas Edison with His Phonograph (left)
Popular Electronics, October 1995 (right)

The 1980s and 1900s: Ghost box origins

The ghost box was first utilized in the early 1980s. The earliest is considered to be "the Spiricom." It was built by a man named William O'Neil, who claimed that he was able to hold two-way communication with the dead. He offered up the plans for his device, and several attempted to recreate his results, with no luck. A little over twenty years later, Frank Sumption was inspired by an October 1995 *Popular Electronics* magazine article that asked, "Are the dead trying to communicate with us through electronic means? Try these experiments and see for yourself." As a result of this he created the "Frank Box." It was essentially an AM radio combined with a white-noise generator. This is much closer to the ghost box we know and love today. While many have used the Frank Box with much better results, critics claim that because of its nature, the results cannot be replicated, and that the radio stations can cause natural voices to be heard.[4]

2007: The Shack Hack ghost box is born

As time passed, the idea evolved into devices that were less complex, cheaper, and easier to make. Perhaps one of the most prevalent of these "next generation" devices was the "Shack Hack." It was created by Bill Chappell on November 24, 2007. He utilized a commonly used Radio Shack 12-469 AM/FM radio that, with minor modifications, become a working ghost box. We have used a variety of devices, and thus far the Shack Hack 12-469 is our favorite. Later, Mike Colletta used the same technique from Bill Chappell's modification to hack the Radio Shack 12-470.

The quirks of ghost boxes

Because we have had experiences with several different boxes, we have learned a few interesting things about them. First, different people prefer different models. Each box has its own personality and quirks that have to which the Listener must be acclimatized. For example, we have two Shack Hack boxes made with different radio models. One has a much faster scan rate than the other. So the Listener experiences a much different session with one box than with the other. Oddly enough, it seems that people with a certain box can receive messages with that particular box, and not with another. Chances are it is because of a person being used to a certain style, and not for a "spiritual" reason. However, there are some who think that a relationship is made with the device itself. Some even maintain that you should keep the box with you, even sleep with it, to maintain such a relationship. While we are not writing a philosophical book on how this could be, it is important to note that there appear to be favorites when it comes to boxes.

In one experiment we had one person use a ghost box that produced a very limited number of responses to questions. This was the case in real-time review and was confirmed even more during evidence review. It was as if the box simply did not work. We then took the same box to the same location but gave it to another person on the team. Instantly, the box sprang to life, with extremely frequent and detailed responses. The only variable that had changed was the Listener. The point here is that a ghost box, unlike typical digital devices, does not perform consistently every time you turn it on. Results will vary depending on when, where, why and who is using it. Many times in going to a location attempting to extract historical facts about the people and events, we have instead walked away completely baffled about the diversity of responses and the lack of expected results. In other words, expectations and ghost boxes don't always go together.

Understanding sweep rate preferences

When choosing a box for your investigations, there are several factors to consider. We find that a radio that flips, or *sweeps*, through the channels faster is better than one that slowly crawls. This is for two reasons. First, a slower radio can linger on a channel for a much longer period of time. This allows for easier contamination by a standard radio station, as you could get full words or phrases from a station instead of a supernatural source. Second, you get more dead space. The time between channels is also longer in a slower scan, which means less material for a spirit to work with. On the other hand, you can purchase boxes that allow you to speed up and slow down this scan rate, so that may be an option for you as well. Again, it comes back to personal style: some people may prefer a slower scan rate, while others are just the opposite. For this reason it may be a good idea to have several ghost boxes in your tool kit.

Disclaimer: Remember the purpose of this book

The purpose of this book is not to provide the technical details about how to build your own box. The internet is littered with documentation to help you in that area. We do, however, want you to be informed about how to find this information in preparation for your own ghost box experiments. Then, in conjunction with the methods discussed in this book, you can conduct successful Double Blind and Triple Blind Ghost Box experiments for yourself.

Purchasing Gary's Ghost Box ITC P-SB7

You can purchase ghost boxes, spirit boxes, or known radios that can be modified (Shack Hacks) on the internet or at electronic equipment stores. One of the scan-rate-adjustable boxes available now is the ITC P-SB7 Spirit Box designed by Gary Galka of D.A.S. Distribution Inc.[5] The P-SB7 Spirit Box was made famous during the Travel Channel's *Ghost Adventures* live broadcast from the Trans-Allegheny Lunatic Asylum in Weston, West Virginia, on October 30, 2009. During the seven-hour lockdown, Chris Fleming, a psychic medium and founder of *Unknown Magazine*, used the P-SB7 to communicate with spirits at the asylum. Up to this point in paranormal TV, onlookers were quite used to "after the fact" revelations of EVP, and not real-time two-way communication. Spectators from all around the world watched in amazement as the box responded to questions posed by Chris and the *Ghost Adventures* team for almost an hour. The P-SB7 Spirit Box is reasonably affordable and requires no manual modifications out of the box in order to work. This is a good choice for your first ghost box and features a wide range of in-the-field-adjustable options. Using this box will also help you calibrate the scan rates that you are most comfortable with, while quickly increasing your knowledge of what the various terms are as they relate to the technology. Ironically, of the boxes we have on our team, this is the least popular. By no means is this because it is an inferior box, but rather because, as you have read, one gets used to a particular box, and once you find "the one," it is hard to let go and learn new ones. Shawn and Dan had to purchase several of the relic boxes to keep the team happy. So, what are the relics?

Purchase or make your own ghost box: *Hacks*

The Radio Shack 12-469 and 12-470 radios are considered to be the original "Shack Hack" ghost boxes. They are no longer in production but are highly desired and valuable. Back in the day they sold for twenty-five dollars at Radio Shack but now sell for over five to seven times that online and unmodified. If you can get your hands on one of these, you will need to research the technical modification needed to convert them into ghost boxes. The good news is that these modifications are not too difficult and are easily found on various internet websites like YouTube. For example, the 12-470 requires only the mute wire to be cut. On the other hand, if you purchase a simple AM/FM radio for $125 and botch the modification, it becomes useless. Another alternative to this would be to purchase a Shack Hack that is already modified. You will pay more for the convenience, but there are fewer risks for the price. Most importantly when it comes to purchasing Shack Hacks, do your homework first. By now you should know all the keywords to search for from this book. *Ghost box, spirit box*, and *Shack Hack* will produce hundreds of results for the Web, video, and sales sites across the world. Also, many of the models out there evolved over time and became "unhackable." The same model distributed in 2008 may look the same in 2011, but on the inside significant changes could have been made. This means that you could buy a specific model on e-Bay only to find that you now have an expensive radio and not one that can be converted to a ghost box. Unfortunately, the 12-470 is one of those models. This is one reason why this book does not focus on how to build a box, and why we have added a disclaimer to its content. Because the technology is changing so fast, we cannot stress enough that you research the boxes that are currently available to you before you waste money and time. You may even want to write down the technical information on how to do the modifications if necessary. Just the other day we purchased an unmodified Shack Hack and found a site to perform the necessary modifications. The box worked great, but when we went back a few days later, the video had been removed and we could not find the plans anywhere. Do not be discouraged, though. As you will discover, there are many boxes available today, and that list is growing exponentially.

Now that we have covered a few of the most notable boxes, here is a quick list of common boxes available online at the time this book was written. Again, *do not* use this book as the purchasing or modification guide for ghost boxes! Make sure you research them in depth before purchasing.

Aiwa HS-TX591   Jensen SAB-55   Koss PP257, PP267   Minibox Plus 515

P-SB7 Spirit Box   Radio Shack 12-469   Radio Shack 12-470   Radio Shack 12-587

Radio Shack 12-820   Radio Shack 20-125   Sangean DT-200VX   Sony SRF-M37Vb

Common Ghost Boxes and Shack Hacks

Chapter Three

The Issues with Today's Ghost Box Methods

Next we want to discuss the theory behind what is believed to be happening. This will help you determine if you should or shouldn't include a ghost box in your repertoire of paranormal tools. As with any tool we use, there is a level of experimentation with everything we do. Although many tools such as EMF detectors are widely accepted, they are still not completely understood and can easily be fooled by natural phenomena. Researchers can also be fooled by false positive EVP caused by the brush of a jacket or faint voices from an adjoining building. So, not unlike its peers, the ghost box stands with its own obvious downsides. However, that is why you are holding this book in your hand. *How can we minimize the downsides of the device to gain the advantages that real-time communication can provide?*

The basic theory: Ghosts use the box to talk

Before we discuss the particulars of the problems facing this device, let's first recap the basic theory on which it stands. As the device scans through the different frequencies, bits and pieces of signals flip through as the channels are passed. As we discussed previously, these frequencies can be altered and the scanning speeds can vary from device to device. The Listener then attempts to pick out responses from the jumbled mess of signals that could be a communication response or initiation from beyond the grave. *The idea here is that an entity can use these bits and pieces to formulate a response.* The way that a message is then extrapolated is that these responses should stand out from the others.

On occasion you will receive responses that seem to originate more like an EVP. In fact, we will give examples later in the book. However, most responses come in *quick bursts* that will be two to three words long. You must be careful about single-syllable words, as they are easily picked out from a radio station, although if they are clear enough it does not hurt to say the word aloud. We find that there is a statistical aspect to this method and that not everything heard is accurate. What you are looking for are responses and not free-floating words. We discuss that further in the technical details of this book.

Nothing more than radio stations and static?

As simple as the process sounds, it has several points that draw the ire of many skeptics and critics alike. The most obvious issue is that most listeners who first hear the ghost box, even with an open mind about the technology, will no doubt say it's nothing more than radio stations zooming by. Technically speaking, this is true. Our claim, with or without the Double Blind Ghost Box process, is that if you ask the question, "What color is the sky?" the answer should be "blue" or whatever the sky color just so happens to be at the time. However, quickly scanning by radio stations could just as easily answer "Papa John's Pizza" at slower scan rates. It is highly likely that at some point you will hear radio commercial blips or portions of songs in the top forty countdown of the week during an investigation. However, remember that *we claim the box is providing a mechanism that an intelligent entity can manipulate in an effort to produce a response or initiate a communication.*

To illustrate this, get a bunch of magazines and stack them one on top of the other. Now flip through the pages while looking at the images as they zoom by. Now have a second person observe these pages zoom by as well. Then ask what color the sky is, and have the second person attempt to select an answer to that question as the pages continue to flip. Assuming the second person is fast enough, he or she would undoubtedly select the first bold-color blue image or even a word. Now imagine that the second person is lightning-fast at making those selections. As you ask questions, they continue to make selections, answering the questions the best they can with the pages they have to work with. This is exactly what is happening with a ghost box. In our example a skeptic would say that there is nothing supernatural at all going on, because the mechanism is merely a stack of magazines. But if you use scientific experiments, such as *a double-blind test,* you could, in time, show enough evidence that there is in fact a second person with lightning-fast reflexes answering questions.

What is facial matrixing?

Another central problem lies with the Listener. Any valid researcher can explain to you the concept of "facial matrixing." The human brain is a fantastic wonder. The only thing that the mind does not like is pure chaos. Facial matrixing occurs when we see a random pattern; our brain tries to make sense of it. For some reason, our mind tries to find facial features in the chaos until we can see a face. Don't believe us? Look at a patch of carpet or a stucco ceiling. You will immediately begin to see different faces. This is one reason that grainy ghost photos have to be scrutinized.

How to combat matrixing

Matrixing can cause enthusiastic paranormal investigators to see a ghost under every rock. To avoid this trap, simply surround yourself in a community of honest investigators, and have them review evidence with you. *Focusing on quality over quantity is the key.* We feel as many researchers do. We are not out there doing our investigations, being so desperate and going as far as to fabricate evidence in an effort to prove there is an afterlife. We know there is an afterlife but are patient to let evidence manifest in its own time. If we wanted to fabricate evidence, we could do that without spending so many sleepless hours investigating, poring through case files, videos, and audio recordings. To us, it is just as much about discovery as it is trying to prove the discovery. We are simply "putting ourselves out there" for the sake of sharing that which we have learned. It is for this reason that we were reluctant to include the ghost box in evidence right away. We were not sure about the technology to begin with, and as such, we had to pull in the scientific method to prove or disprove its effectiveness for ourselves first.

Real-world example of facial matrixing

Most people by now have heard of the famous "Christ on Toast" sold on eBay. This was a classic case of matrixing, where people saw the face of Christ on a piece of toast. We will demonstrate a more complex example of matrixing in the form of a stereogram. In the image named "Matrixing the Dragon Army," we took a photograph of the clouds overlooking a battleground. We took the picture because we could clearly see in the clouds an army of warriors on horseback while a dragon flew over their heads. Of course there was not really an army in the sky, and especially not a dragon. In reality our imagination took the chaos within the clouds of the sky and transformed it into something our minds could relate to. The reason we chose to render this image as a stereogram is so that you can see the figures more prominently in three dimensions.

Stereogram: Matrixing the Dragon Army

Although you may already see the figures simply by looking at the image directly, to see the results of the stereogram in 3-D, look at the image and relax your eyes on the two dots at the bottom until they form four dots. Then slowly relax your eyes more, allowing the four dots to drift toward each other until finally they become three dots. When that happens the image will pop to life off the page, and you will see the figures defined in three dimensions. In the image "The Dragon Army Revealed," we have outlined the figures for you. There is nothing supernatural going on here. It is simply a natural phenomenon of the human mind.

The Dragon Army Revealed

Audio matrixing

The ghost box presents the same issue as facial matrixing, but with a twist. We call it "audio matrixing." As questions are asked, the Listener tries to pull out answers from the noise of the ghost box signals. Even though the radio is flying through the channels, single-syllable words can easily be heard. For example, if the question is "Are you a female?" then the Listener knows to listen for a "yes" or "no" response. Due to this anticipation, the answer can easily be "matrixed," pulled out, and a yes or no response given. Unfortunately, this is called a false positive even if by chance it may have been a correct answer. Going back to the magazine-flipping illustration, because the Questioner asked, "What color is the sky?" *they themselves are looking at the magazine expecting the answer to be "Blue."* They see just about every blue item that zooms by. The answering party may have chosen "black," but the Questioner was so fixated on an expected answer that he or she matrixed "blue." This is similar to the *Stroop test,* where reaction times and error rates increase when a person is asked to read the name of a color written in a different color. The mind can play tricks because it is trying to make order out of the chaos it sees or hears. *This is where the Double and Triple Blind Ghost Box process will shine: by reducing these false positives.* Granted, these processes will not eliminate matrixing. Remember, matrixing is a natural function of the brain. There will be more on this topic later.

A desperate Listener

Related to this matrixing issue is the stress that the Listener can be under. You want desperately to communicate, so it is easy to create an entire conversation based on responses that the Listeners themselves are creating unknowingly.

Using speakers or headphones

When you look for videos where the ghost box is being used, you will commonly observe that the box is *connected to speakers.* It is highly likely that the first few words on the screen will be something like "Please use headphones while watching/ listening to this video." This is because ghost box audio is best heard using headphones. As you will discover in the technical details behind the Double Blind Ghost Box process, the use of headphones is a key element, but for very different reasons. The issue here is that the Questioner and/or Listener in the video is listening to the box in conjunction with the *ambiance of the environment* they are in. *Using headphones is the best way to listen to ghost box output.* Listening in a quiet room would be next-best option. The worst-case scenario would be to listen to a ghost box output with distractions in the room or in the field. You would not believe how often and to what degree these distractions can affect what is heard. To combat this we have established techniques to isolate all audio variables of a ghost box experiment. You will learn how to set this up in simple to more complex configurations so that each portion can be analyzed individually or in conjunction with others during evidence reviews.

Too many flaws without a scientific control

The aforementioned are just a few reasons why ghost box experiments can be flawed if not done in a more methodical way. That is why this book has been written. We are attempting to take a "loose cannon" technology and apply it in such a way that true communication can be had, if it exists. We will discuss the methodology used to perform a Double Blind and Triple Blind Ghost Box experiment, and show you how to process the information you receive. So without any further delays, we present to you the double-blind process.

CHAPTER FOUR

Conducting an Objective Ghost Box Experiment

In this chapter we discuss in detail how to perform a Double Blind and Triple Blind ghost Box session. In a normal ghost box session, you typically see a few folks standing around a ghost box that is connected to external speakers. They ask questions and any responses that come through the box are heard by everyone around it. In the previous chapters we covered extensively why this method of ghost box sessions is flawed. It has its place, but the purpose of this book is to show you how to take a subjective tool and apply as many objective scientific methods as possible to prove or disprove a hypothesis.

Fundamentals of double-blind experiments

The most fundamental purpose of the Double Blind Ghost Box session is to produce a situation in which a Questioner asks questions that the Listener cannot hear. Meanwhile, the Listener repeats words and phrases heard from the ghost box. If the Listener answers the questions correctly, without any knowledge of what those questions are, then you are accomplishing the statistically impossible. If the theory is that a spirit without a physical body is in some way able to use the ghost box device to communicate, this double-blind method is a valid test to prove or disprove that theory.

Key roles: Questioner and Listener

To conduct a Double Blind Ghost Box session, you will have at the very least two key roles in this experiment: the Questioner and the Listener. The Listener will have a ghost box, a headset, and two recorders. They will connect the ghost box (audio out) to the (mic input on the) first recorder (this is called the ghost box recorder). Then the Listener will connect the headset to the headset jack on the ghost box recorder. The second recorder will be used to record the Listener's voice (this is called the Listener's mic recorder) during the experiment.

Double Blind Ghost Box Configuration

GB   GBR   L1R

In this formation the ghost box will send audio through the first recorder (GBR) and into the Listener's headset (L1HS), allowing the second mic recorder (L1R) to hear only the Listener, and not the ghost box audio. This way you can separate the ghost box audio from the Listener's responses during evidence review.

Triple Blind Ghost Box Configuration

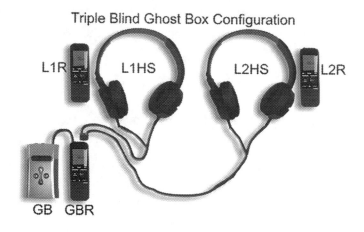

Triple Blind Ghost Box experiments would have one Questioner, one ghost box, and two Listeners splitting the same ghost box. In this way there are two Listeners potentially saying the same words from the ghost box. If they do not have the same response, this assists in the evaluation of potential matrixed words. You can also have one Listener and two separate double-blind configurations running simultaneously. Remember, this is science, so mix it up, graph it, and hypothesize!

Setting the ghost box volume correctly

Before the experiment begins, the Listener will turn on the ghost box and its recorder, turning the recorder volume up about halfway. The Listener turns the ghost box volume down all the way and slowly raises the volume until there is a solid stream of clear sound. This avoids overdriving the recorder's microphone, which would destroy the ghost box recorder's audio file quality during evidence review. Overdriving the audio from the ghost box causes upper-range clipping damage of responses. From there, the Questioner starts speaking some test phrases while the Listener slowly turns up the volume (on the ghost box recorder) until he or she can no longer hear the

Questioner. The idea here is to use the recorder's volume to drown out all external sounds, with only the ghost box audible. The volume should be at a comfortable but effective level. Note that some recorders will allow you to hear the ghost box audio-out only while you are recording or recording and paused. Some recorders do not support simultaneous audio in and out. Obviously, you will not be able to use that type of recorder for this experiment. With these preparations made, you are set to go. Let's get this experiment rolling!

Critical markers: 3, 2, 1 mark audio/video

To begin, all recording devices are turned on and recording started. The Listener now temporarily disconnects the ghost box recorder's (mic in) line while the Questioner and/or Listener conducts a verbal countdown of "3, 2, 1 mark audio" and maybe does a recap of time, location, etc. The point here is that when the session begins, all recording devices must record this "mark audio" statement. The Listener now reconnects the ghost box recorder (mic in) line and hears only the ghost box, at which time the Questioner can begin his or her inquiries.

The Listener during the experiment

The Listener should not look at the Questioner, so as to avoid reading his or her lips or getting any hints a question was asked. The Listener should simply repeat out loud any recognizable words heard. At first, hearing distinct voices through the scrambled mess may be a bit unnerving and difficult. The Listener will need to try to focus and "get into the groove." The Listener will need to inform the Questioner and any observers if she or he hears any external contamination, for example, a question being asked. If that happens, then someone is standing too close to the Listener. Sometimes spirits may pull the Listener verbally or, in extreme cases, even physically. Be sure to communicate this to those conducting the experiment.

The Questioner during the experiment

It is usually a good idea for the Questioner to have a prepared list of questions that the Listener has no awareness of. However, as stated before, do not be disappointed if that list of questions does not get answered. For example, let's say you are investigating the house of a now-deceased military general. One could logically ask questions about the general, the life he led, aspects of the time in which he lived, and so on. But the box may not get responses from the general. Instead it may produce responses from a completely different time period or from other spirits in the area. We call this the layering, or levels of time, in the field of the paranormal. A good Questioner should be able to pick up on this and reasonably adapt to, redirect, and/ or refocus the dialog.

Disclaimer: The Questioner is responsible for safety

This brings us to another key point about the role of a Questioner. Be sure that the Questioner drives the conversation, and not the other way around. If you are dealing with a true intelligence, then the conversation should be reciprocal. If you are dealing with *residual phenomena*, then it will be like talking to a broken record, quite literally. Residual phenomena is a state by which a period of time is repeated over and over. Entities in such a loop will not respond to questions and will not offer any sign that they know you are there.

Instead of going through long-winded examples of productive and nonproductive communication, we will simply say here that the Questioner needs to keep control of the conversation and not run down rabbit holes. Speaking of rabbit holes, it is also the Questioner's responsibility to protect and guide the Listener, so that he or she does not literally fall into a rabbit hole or a ditch, or get hit by an oncoming car. We say this because in some experiments the Questioner and/or Listener may be led to move to another location. In some cases the Listener may choose to close his or her eyes in order to filter the minutiae to find intelligent words or phrases. At times you may choose to conduct a ghost box experiment in the dark or in an old, abandoned building. All these situations put the Listener at risk, because in most cases, the Listener can't see or hear the surrounding world at times during the experiment. The Questioner and observers should be aware of these risks, and all should be prepared and highly aware at all times.

In one experiment we conducted, the Questioner used a laser pointer on the ground to guide the movements of the Listener. Moreover, the Questioner would tap the Listener on the shoulder to get the Listener's attention for some specific instructions. It is also a good idea to have the Questioner or an observer video-record the experiment from start to finish without stopping the recording.

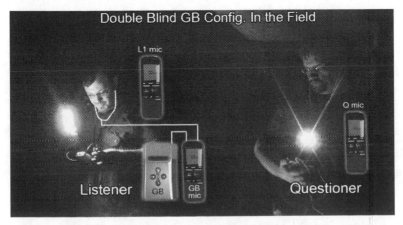

Shawn Taylor (Listener) and Dan Morgan (Questioner) Double Blind Ghost Box configuration while in the field.

Double Blind Ghost Box method recap

In most ghost box experiments seen on the Web or television, you will observe that the Questioner is also the Listener. We discussed the issues with this configuration in chapter 3. In the Double and Triple Blind configurations, the Questioner and Listener are two different people. Again, in this configuration the Listener cannot hear or see the Questioner's inquiries. In this image Dan (on the right) is the Questioner. He has an audio amplification application running so he can hear a pin drop in the room while asking questions. In some cases there will be sounds detected in the environment that correspond with the questions and answers. The official Listener would not be able to detect audio anomalies in the environment during the experiment. Dan also has a designated Questioner mic positioned in a hands-free location. Shawn (on the left) is the Listener. He has a 12-769 Shack Hack in his hand connected to a designated ghost box mic, and a headset on so he can hear only the ghost box responses. He has a designated Listener mic positioned in a hands-free location.

Mary Russell (Listener1) and Shawn Taylor (Listener2)
Triple Blind Ghost Box configuration in the field

To recap, the Listener sets up the equipment in such a way as to not overdrive the audio from the ghost box. The Listener then sets the recorder volume high enough not to hear the Questioner. The Listener also avoids eye contact with the Questioner and generally avoids any means of detecting that questions are being asked. The Listener and/or Questioner verbally marks all recording devices with the "mark audio" cue. The Listener's job is to listen for any recognizable words or phrases and to repeat them the best he or she can. The Questioner should be prepared with questions, protect the Listener from dangers, and drive the experiment intelligently. One more thing! Make sure you start with fresh batteries in all devices. It is ideal to have one file (end to end) from each recording device. This will make it much easier to line up the files during evidence review.

CHAPTER FIVE

Processing Ghost Box Evidence

The key files

When conducting a Double Blind Ghost Box session you will have at the very least three files for evidence review. These files are:

1. The video file
2. The Listener's mic recorder file
3. The ghost box recorder file

You may want to add a Questioner's mic recorder, but this is not required if the Questioner is also the person with the video recorder.

Lining up the files

One of the prevalent issues with compiling ghost box evidence is lining up these three files correctly. This becomes exceedingly difficult when different devices have different recording/playback speeds. So make sure you use the same make and model for the Listener's mic recorder and the ghost box recorder. For example, in 2012 our team used the Sony ICD-

PX312, which allows you to record the ghost box output while attaching the Listener's headset with ease. These recorders also line up perfectly with the audio playback speed of our video cameras.

To best line up the three files, first turn on all three recorders without the ghost box recorder being linked to the ghost box. The Questioner and/or Listener will then conduct a verbal countdown of "3, 2, 1 mark audio" and maybe do a recap of time, location etc. The point here is that when the session begins, all recording devices must record this "mark audio" statement. Once the session is over, the Questioner and/ or Listener will then make another statement like "End ghost box session alpha." Without audio start/stop markers, you will have trouble lining up the files during evidence review.

Also be sure that your recorders are not in Automatic Voice Recording (AVR) mode, which records only when you are speaking into the microphone. AVR mode can significantly misalign your files. Finally, you want to be sure to record the entire session without any breaks, any pausing or stopping of the devices. Any stops in audio or video will cause more work when it comes time to line up these files. Once you import your files into video editing software (such as Sony Vegas), all you have to do is listen for the start/stop markers and confirm both start and stop markers align perfectly.

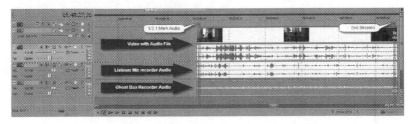

Evidence Files Alignment

Being a good Listener is not easy

While in the field the primary role of the Listener is to listen for any recognizable words, sounds, or phrases heard on the ghost box and speak them aloud. As you can imagine, the Listener can:

1. Miss ghost box responses to questions altogether.
2. Mishear and/or speak the wrong response from the box.
3. Speak a response too soon and, as a result, miss parts of a phrased response. (For example, if the full response was, "I am Lieutenant Colonel John Doe McMurdoch," but the Listener hears the first half of the phrase and speaks, "I am Lieutenant Colonel," by the time they end the statement they've lost the second half of the phrase. Not to mention that most Listeners would not even pick up on the "John Doe McMurdoch" part of the phrase. At the very best, a seasoned Listener would hear, "I am Lieutenant Colonel John Doe.")
4. Wait too long to process a response and either forget the first response because a second is now speaking or decide not to mention it at all and move on.

In the field, real-time ghost box listening is not easy. Even a seasoned Listener can miss or incorrectly speak a response quite easily. Triple Blind configurations may help with this by giving the Questioner and observer two Listeners to evaluate in real time.

Advantages of using separate audio files

This is why we don't just do the real-time session and depend completely on what the video records the Questioner and Listeners saying. Lining up the video recording with the Listener and ghost box recording gives you some advantages during evidence review. In this section we will reference the Sony Vegas as the tool being used to align and assist with the evidence review. Keep in mind there are many other video editing tools out there that can do this effectively, but our team uses Vegas. Once you have the files aligned, you have such luxuries as:

1. Hearing the full context of the conversation.
2. Muting the ghost box and hearing just the Questioner and Listener.
3. Muting the Listener and hearing just the Questioner and ghost box.
4. Muting the Questioner and hearing just the ghost box and Listener.
5. Selecting a specific time range of ghost box audio and "looping" it so you can hear the responses over and over, something the Listener in the field can't do.
6. Muting or cutting out distracting ghost box sweeping noise.
7. Exporting, cleaning up, and/or enhancing the audio as needed.

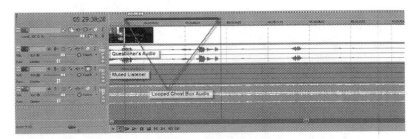

Benefits of Video and Audio Editing Software

The intention of a Double Blind Ghost Box session is that

the Listener does not know what the questions are and thus can't matrix or look for a response. You can verify this dynamic with the video footage alone, but during evidence review you can now take a closer, more scrupulous look at all points of view.

Time is not on your side

The downside to these luxuries is that in most cases time is not on your side. Most clients want evidence revealing as soon as possible. They are thinking of processing in terms of days and weeks. This is in opposition to true evidence review and processing of ghost box materials, which can take weeks to months. With all this data at your disposal, if you are not mindful about your time management, you could get stuck in analysis paralysis. We can't tell you how many times we ran out of time on reviews because of overlapping investigations and priorities snuffing out much-needed deep dives into sessions. You will no doubt wish you had more time, especially once you get your clientele built up.

Evidence reviewers can matrix too

Another downside is that evidence reviewers who have the luxury of the "full context" can also matrix responses based on the Questioner's queries. To combat this, be sure to pull in others to review the evidence, to confirm that what you are hearing is also accepted by the team. Again, the focus of this process is to take a subjective tool and apply as many objective scientific methods as possible to prove or disprove a hypothesis. The solipsism hypothesis would be, "Nothing beyond myself, *the physical*, exists," right?[1] Seriously, if you do this the right way, the result *will stun you*! We both went into this field believing that the ghost box was simply another matrix-generating tool that we could debunk in a few sessions. After a few simple controlled experiments, we were both standing with our mouths open, finding that our previous beliefs were completely wrong. It is equivalent to thinking it's impossible for man to fly and then seeing the Wright Brothers zoom over your head, laughing all the way into the history books.

Cleaning up annoying sweep noise

At this point you may have noticed that the ghost box recorder produces a bunch of annoying sounds with responses mixed in. You also may notice that at times you get responses at the same time the Questioner and/or the Listener is speaking. Evidence review is also the time to start cleaning up the responses so that you get a smooth question-and-answer flow for the investigation. If you are using a Sony Vegas, this means that you clip out the sweep noise, leaving only the ghost box responses. You may need to shift the response a bit, so it does not get mixed with Questioner/Listener speaking. Be sure to save your source files, because skeptics will no doubt be wanting further proof of the event. We would prefer to leave responses exactly where they fall in the sequence of a session. However, in reality you have to present the evidence so that people can clearly hear the questions and the true response in a timely fashion. If you have the responses all mixed up between the Questioner and Listener speaking, your client may not hear the most important parts of the session which are the "responses to questions." This in itself is another drawback to the process; a deceptive evidence reviewer could twist responses and in essence fabricate a desired outcome. Again, save your source files, pull in team members during reviews, and consider the full context of the session to help in these cases. The point of this book is to give you an objective way to use a very subjective tool for the pursuit of truth in the paranormal field. If you are looking to fabricate evidence, just remember that if you give this process a chance, it will prove itself true. Leave fabrication to the immature, and strive for truth. The ghost box, when used correctly, will not disappoint you.

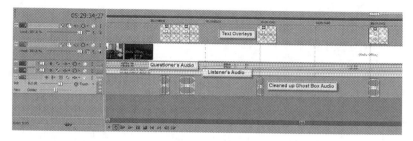

Cleaning up ghost box sweeping noise

Add text overlays

When presenting your evidence as a video, it is a good practice to include text overlays that show what the ghost box or EVP said. Most video editing software packages have this feature available.

Proper enhancement practices

In some cases the response from a ghost box may require the evidence reviewer to export a portion of the audio file to an external audio editing software package. This allows the reviewer to perform functions such as noise removal, gain, etc. Usually, ghost box responses do not need this type of transformation. Yet, if you do run into this need, we recommend that you present the original clip first and then replay it in the enhanced version. You would use this same technique for EVP cleanup and/or enhancements for presentations.

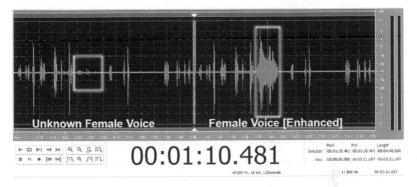

Enhanced audio before and after

Other cleanup/review ideas: Reverse and aging

In one case the response was played in reverse, which produced an extremely clear phrase that stunned everyone. So having external audio editing tools available is highly recommended. Another cleanup/review enhancing technique is, ironically, to replay the original recordings days, weeks, months, or even years later. This is called aging. Sometimes when you are in the middle of a long evidence review, you hear responses at that time and choose to set them aside for the reveal. Then you come back a day later and hear even more responses that you missed the previous day, so you add them in as well. The recordings can "age" and reveal more evidence over time. We know that the recordings themselves may not be truly aging or maturing over time, like an old Polaroid photo. Still, fresh eyes and ears over time can be rewarding.

Use a headset and keep it quiet

When reviewing ghost box evidence, you will want to use a good headset connected to your computer and make sure the room is quiet. Here is why: ambient noise and sounds in the room will affect what you hear and how you interpret ghost box responses. For example, you have a TV on in the room, and you hear a response on the box and also hear the TV. In that case what you hear is not the truth, but a distortion, a contaminated subject. You play it back and don't hear the same thing. So you are introducing contamination into your evidence review process and wasting valuable time. The idea is to keep the evidence review clean and contamination-free, and everything you see and hear is at its best output levels. One would not want to open a Petri dish with a perfect specimen in it while colleagues are sneezing all around it!

Things to remember (the cheat sheet)

In this section we provide tips for processing the evidence from a ghost box session.

- Use common makes and models of recorders that sync well with video recorders.
- Always verbally mark audio/video starts and stops: "3, 2, 1 mark audio."
- Leave devices rolling, no pausing, and turn off AVR modes.
- Use a good software package to handle the lining up of all the files from the session.
- Remove sweep noise and align files for a smooth question-and-answer playback for your clients.
- When enhancing audio be sure to play the original version first, then play the enhanced version.
- Revisit the sessions over time; allow the recordings to age and reveal more responses.
- During evidence reviews use a good headset and keep the room quiet. *No contaminations.*
- Trust that this ghost box phenomenon will do its part and produce evidence if you use it correctly.

- Keep your original source files! You never know when you will need them.

Expect long hours and late nights doing evidence reviews.

CHAPTER SIX

Spirits: The Good, Bad, and Ugly

Now, before we release you to the new world of Double Blind Ghost Box experiments of your own, we want to give you an idea of what you may encounter while in the field. If you read through the transcripts in chapter 9, you will catch a glimpse into the wide variety of spirits that you may interact with. By no means will this book or the transcripts prepare you for everything you may encounter. The purpose of this book is to cover the double-blind process specifically. However, we do not want you to jump into this without covering the bases, even if on a basic level. Chapter 9 outlines some of our most notable experiences, and in no way is limited to the basics, so we believe it should be enough to give you a good idea about what to expect. With that said, we encounter new situations that often make us scratch our heads, ponder for a few days or weeks, and at times beckon us to rethink. So will you. This chapter will act as a basic guide to two primary spirit categories (human and nonhuman), which you will get an opportunity to read about in the transcripts. We do not intend to offer any philosophical understanding in this book, and any that may be implied should be seen only as general observations. This book is about the process and not what we believe. We have included conversations and observations in a way of validating the Double Blind Process. We will discuss our own beliefs in another book.

Choice of terms

When employing the use of a ghost box, there are several different types of entities you may encounter. Most of these are widely recognized in paranormal circles as existing but are called by a variety of different names. In this chapter we will use terms/names commonly accepted across paranormal and non-paranormal fields alike. When real-time communication is used, these spirits or "personalities" become more prevalent but can sometimes be hard to discern. Once during a ghost box session we were told, "Be careful who you talk to; there are some that would be out to destroy you."

Know who you are talking with

Identifying the "who" on the other end of the box can sometimes be a difficult task. Think for a moment about a conversation you might have in an open forum in an online chat. There are four participants, including yourself. You have never met any of them before and know only what is offered up online. You spend the better part of an hour getting to know each one. You speak to a girl named Girl007, a retired schoolteacher called Teach4kids, and a twenty-something called OnTheHunt. You learn that Girl007 is sixteen and just got her driver's license. Teach4kids retired a couple of years ago, and his wife died in a tragic car accident last year. OnTheHunt is looking for a date and asks you several questions related to this quest. After an hour you feel like you know each one and have a good feel for who each is and why each is there. However, beneath the surface lies the truth: Girl007 is actually a forty-year-old man who lives in his parents' basement, Teach4kids is what he says he is, and OnTheHunt is a ten-year-old boy having fun on his parents' computer.

Things may not be what they appear

Obviously, when dedicating time with someone, the desire is to know who it is that you are talking with. But so often you have no way of knowing the truth about someone unless you know how to look for subtle clues during the conversation. Include the variations of personalities and motives, and the results can become exceedingly difficult to interpret. A "ghost" you are speaking to named Annie may in fact be a demon named Bob. "Knowing the spirit" is not new to paranormal research, but this is where a ghost box can help shine a light on the subject at hand. With the ghost box you can use real-time interrogation techniques to increase your ability to discern who it is you are speaking to.

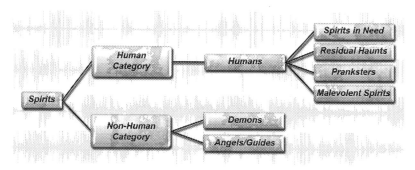

A Basic Spirit Tree

Human spirits

In the many investigations where we have utilized the double-blind method, we have observed two major categories of entities (human and nonhuman), and three primary types (humans, demons, angels/guides), each with a diversity of subtypes. The most common and, in most cases, the target group would be the "human spirit" category, or, more traditionally, "ghosts." These are spirits who once lived as we do today, but for whatever reasons are still here after their death. We dare not say "trapped," because in some cases there is an *active choice* to remain. This is by far the most diverse group we have encountered. This makes sense; the diversity found in personalities in life would logically be displayed by human spirits. Countless observations to date substantiate the idea that personality and/or individuality is retained after death.

Spirits in need

Speaking with human spirits who do not wish to be in their current situation is a common experience. These "spirits in need" usually attempt to communicate by pleading for help. It is such a common occurrence that one wonders if they spend every waking moment drifting around asking for help from those who cannot even hear them. Whether or not this is the case, many of these spirits will attempt communication on some level. It is not an uncommon occurrence for this subtype to go right on asking for help even after you offer it. It is almost as if they are suffering from a type of insanity and can only repeat themselves after asking for so long.

The responses of those human spirits who do grasp the offer of help are usually frantic. They are so desperate for the help they seek that they have a sense of urgency about them. These generally have no idea of where they are (or why they are). They are simply afraid and wish to be someplace else. Other human spirits have a vague awareness but have no clue of how to "move on."

Residual haunts

Another subtype of human spirit may or may not be a sentient spirit at all. These are commonly referred to as "residual haunts." The theory floating around many paranormal circles is that these are not so much spirits as energies left by strong emotions. If this theory holds true, the energy could even be from a person who is still alive! Our experience tells us that these may be spirits who do not have the ability to communicate on any level. We run into these from time to time, as they speak but seem to be of a mind that we, the living in the body, do not exist. If these spirits are aware of themselves, then saying they are "in denial" may not be too strong of an assessment. You can liken these spirits to Sisyphus, who was doomed to roll a huge stone up a hill only to watch it fall down for him to roll back up again and again, forever.

Residual haunting spirits are difficult, if not impossible, to contact using the double-blind method. This is because the spirit does not respond to questions. For this reason the double-blind process is rendered ineffective and therefore not employed for residual haunts. The only way to detect one through the box is by analyzing the recordings and listening for repeating patterns in speech or subject matter. This type of spirit really falls outside the scope of this method, although you may run across some from time to time.

Prankster spirits

Another common human subtype is the "prankster." This type of spirit can be frustrating for a researcher. They usually try to distract or to interfere with experiments, and they tend to masquerade as another spirit or as another type of entity altogether. Our most famous one was a spirit that went by the name of Ed. He kept saying he was a demon, and that he wanted us to leave. We had encountered demons before, and this spirit did not fit the profile. After a longer conversation, we discovered that he was a human spirit that wanted to be something more. Ed followed us the whole night, constantly annoying any researcher that gave him any allowance to communicate.

Malevolent spirits

Another subtype of the traditional human ghost is what

we refer to as the "malevolent spirit." These are by far the most discouraging and the most complicated to deal with. They are generally strong-willed and defiant, and they "bully" other spirits into submission. They have, in several cases, stopped all communication entirely when they find they cannot run the show. In many cases they are difficult to chase out, since they are not demons, and they look for a way to bully the researcher. You will also find that these spirits may sometimes come and go, especially if you have multiple teams on the same location. They do not have the ability to be in two places at once, and they often try to control multiple conversations by going from place to place to maintain their control during the investigation. This is one of their weaknesses that can be used to your advantage. For example, if you have several spirits in need being bullied by a malevolent spirit, you can draw the attention of the one while another other team helps the others.

Nonhuman spirits

The next major category we will discuss is the *"nonhuman spirits."* These are entities that do not have a "former identity" on Earth and exist in the spiritual realm alone. These come in two varieties.

Demons

The first subtype is the "demon." Demons are widely accepted as an entities that any paranormal team may encounter. Many investigative teams are not comfortable with dealing with this type of spirit, and if you are not, this book will not prepare you for that. We strongly urge that no communication be continued if you encounter one.

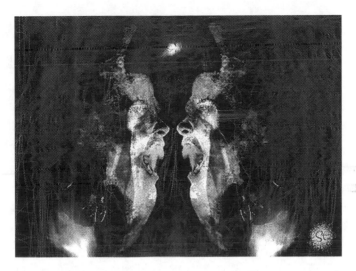

Demons will often attempt to use deception, either in getting you to trust them or in luring you into a trap. They have been known to follow investigators home and even engage in possessions. Some would argue that malevolent spirits would fall into this subtype. However, though demons can manifest as malevolent entities, we make a distinction between human malevolent spirits and nonhuman malevolent demons because they are handled in completely different manners. Often a demon will masquerade as a human, even a human child, entity to get you into a conversation. They are highly manipulative and in no way have your long-term best interests in mind. Submitting to their requests or allowing them to interact with you is only asking for trouble. There are plenty of books and mentors to assist you in the area of demonology.

Angels/Guides

The final subtype that we wish to outline is a type that is difficult to classify. They are sometimes called "angels" or "guides," depending on the beliefs of those discussing them.

These spirits are discernible through their interactions, as other sprits are. However, we have observed that their communication skills through the ghost box are quite advanced, to say the least. Most nonhuman entities are able to come through the box much more clearly and sometimes can speak in complete sentences without pause. The "guides" normally interact directly with the team and will offer advice and help. For example, the "know who you are talking to" advice came from a guide who made the statement and then left the team alone to continue experiments. The only entity we have ever spoken with in this category, "John," spends most of his time speaking with the other spirits and rarely responds to us unless it is absolutely critical.

You should be comfortable in "testing a spirit" before engaging any human or nonhuman entity. Demons masquerade as both humans and angels, and unless you know what to look for you, you could be unwittingly entertaining the will of a demon. In short, it can be difficult to discern the different types and subtypes of spirits and generally should be avoided unless you are experienced. We will cover topics like this in much more detail in a future book. Our intention here in chapter 6 is to provide you with the basics about the various types of spirits that are observed through the ghost box.

CHAPTER SEVEN

Future Ghost Box Science, Tech, and Applications

We almost did not add this chapter, because it is a bit risky to attempt to predict the future. This is especially true when it comes to technology. However, we feel that there is enough information available to point the way and allow us to make an informed guess.

The body of evidence

With the popularity of the paranormal field exploding over the last five years, it is highly likely that it will continue to grow exponentially over the next five to ten years. With the advent of paranormal reality television, the goals to help people feel safer and talk about their own personal experiences with the paranormal have been and will continue to be realized. More paranormal investigative teams have formed and will continue to pop up all over the world, each with its own unique style and niche in the field. Aside from the ghost box device and various tools being used in the field, there is a much more important event being birthed, which overarches the entire topic. The elephant in the room is the growing body of evidence for supernatural anomalies everywhere. At some point the term "fringe science" will not be applied as liberally as it is today. We will see more scientists already notable from many different specialized fields participating in and conducting experiments related to the field of the paranormal. We may even be witness to the slow crumbling of the solipsism view that "nothing beyond the physical exists." The point here is that we will see more evidence using science and by notable scientists in the field as fears and taboos diminish into history.

More facts and more fiction

With the hopes of building a more scientific future for the field, there is also an assurance that destructive fraud will also increase. A few years back there was a video online of a woman sitting in a chair against the wall during an investigation. Suddenly the woman's eyes did that cartoon thing of looking like they were about to pop out of her head. She screamed as she and the chair she was in skittered across the floor, as the rest of the team looked in amazement. The video was a fraud and was caught by another investigator who showed how her elbow pushed against the wall, demonstrating the laws of motion and not the paranormal. Fraudulent and/or purposely misleading evidence like this does more harm to the field of the paranormal than does any other activity, including silly immaturity. Even serious investigators have to let go a little and have some youthful snipe-hunting excursions just to break with the "Why so serious?" face we see on Thomas Edison in chapter 2. Willful deception is the biggest enemy this field has. It will rip away the field's credibility and turn off the scientific community we are depending on to take it to the next levels in its evolution. Enough said.

Will the future be 'Double Blind'?

So let's get back to the topic at hand: the future of the ghost box. We doubt that the immediate future will see a huge explosion of paranormal investigators using the Double Blind and Triple Blind Ghost Box process. Let's face it: it is easier to simply plug in speakers, ask questions, and matrix whatever response you want to hear. It's not science but it's easy.

Granted, we would love to know whether you have learned a great deal from this book and find our process to be an instrumental reference that you carry on every investigation. The only way this methodology can produce the true scientific benefit to the field is for you to share it *when* you find that it works as it did for us. When you discover a true supernatural event that you can test over and over in a controlled fashion, you are adding to the body of evidence that will change perspectives about the world beyond the physical. We are basically handing that opportunity to you on a silver platter. It is up to you to choose what you will do with it.

Technology advancements will be the future

If the immediate future is not the revolution of the Double Blind Ghost Box, most assuredly the maturity of the box will come in the form of technology over process. The basic technology behind the box is simply to scan frequencies without stopping. More work will be pioneered by people like Gary Galka, who gave box users the ability to control the sweep rates, volume, and band and frequency ranges. We will see features like the ability to control the amount of white noise heard from the box. We will see modules added to the ghost box, such as built-in recorders, and even voice-to-text capability. The holy grail of ghost boxes, of course, is the one that allows for fluid communication through the veil, but something tells me we have a way to go for that one. Again, in looking back since the advent of the Shack Hack in 2007, we have not seen much change in the process by which ghost boxes are used. What *has* changed is the device itself and its availability. In hindsight we would have purchased every 12-469 and 12-470 we could, because they sell for five to seven times their value these days.

So we embark on the next chapter in the evolution of paranormal research. As the technology available in our society improves, so will the techniques used to study the supernatur/.al. We are sure that the future for the ghost box is a bright one. In the beginning we thought there was nothing to it but chattering radio stations. After giving it a chance to prove its case, we came to believe that this box, in conjunction with the Double-Blind process, is a leading contender for the tool that will ultimately prove that *something beyond the physical exists*, after all.

Chapter Eight

Conclusions for the Not-So-Faint of Heart

So, as is said in countless crime dramas, "We rest our case." Now you, the jury, must deliberate and determine for yourself if the idea of the double-blind ghost box is a mere delusion or a valid tool, worthy of your own toolbox of paranormal toys and methods. As stated in the beginning of this book, we are not out to prove ourselves. We simply offer what we believe we have seen and experienced, and offer to you the same opportunity, that you may discover for yourself its validity.

No matter what you believe concerning this device, the popularity of these boxes is growing. More and more paranormal videos appear online every day, revealing what they believe to be evidence of life after death. As popularity grows, so will abuses, fakery, and general misunderstanding of the device. The world needs skeptics, but we need open-minded skeptics who are willing, after every precaution is taken and every attempt is made to ensure the process as empirical as possible, to reach the conclusion that what they experience could be paranormal.

We also want to speak to those who are a bit squeamish

about the paranormal. The ghost box is not for the faint of heart. We don't want to be melodramatic and claim that this is the only way you can communicate with the dead. However, the whole process can be very unnerving. One of the most common complaints after a session is that the Listener feels drained. It takes intense concentration to use this method, as the Listener may sometimes need to listen for the soft voices underneath a world of static. When voices begin to come across in this way, the feeling of being alone can be amplified, because there is one focal Listener. At this point, a Listener may feel like the center of attention in what seems to be a room full of entities.

So what does the future of this technology hold for the ghost box? Only time will tell. We believe that as this technology becomes more widely accepted, that more and more devices will be developed for this specific application. We discussed in detail the future of this tool and methods in chapter seven. With the ability to expand the range and static dampening to lessen the background noise, it will be easier to hear voices coming through. The only downside we see is that as we stated earlier, each box is different. You may purchase a box and it does nothing for you where someone else may have better results from the same box. We hope to attempt to understand the reasons behind the pairing phenomenon, but until then purchasing boxes is a shot in the dark as far as results.

As we wrap up this book, we understand that the many philosophical points of this method, like many others, could be debated until the end of time. Some see this method as equal to Ouija boards or divination, while others see it as purely scientific. No matter which school of thought you find yourself aligning with, we hope you can come to the same conclusion we have: this method works. We approached this with a very critical look and came away believers in the technology. Rest assured that we use this in every investigation in some capacity to attempt to ascertain the presence and nature of entities at a location. As you try this, try also to keep an open mind. This does not mean there is a ghost in every static bump you may hear; but truly and objectively listen to what is happening. On occasion you may not get any coherent conversation at all. Words may be pulled out of the noise only to be "matrixed" words from the Listener. That is to be expected. Even during a true conversation this happens from time to time. As Listeners become trained and experienced, they can begin to lessen these "false positives." The point is to experiment and see for yourself if the double-blind ghost box is the method that works for you.

CHAPTER NINE

The Best of Team SAI's Ghost Box Transcripts

The Ghost in Room 302

During the Ramsey Middle School investigation in Bluefield, West Virginia, we conducted an experiment using three devices simultaneously. We did this in an effort to determine whether there was any synergy between them and reported spirits at that location. The three devices were an EMF detector, a Shack Hack 12-467 ghost box, and an experimental smartphone application that we were looking into as a potential device for our tool kit. We will refer to that application as the "GR Words." In this experiment we instructed the spirit to respond using the EMF detector, making it blink once for "Yes" and twice for "No." The Listener was using the ghost box while the Questioner and Observer/s interacted with the spirits in room 302. The experiment began with questions based on earlier evidence that a person may have fallen to their death in the building.

Questioner: Did you fall and hurt yourself here? Once for yes, twice for no. You fell?
EMF Detection: Blinks once: Yes.

GR Words: Slipped, three.

Questioner: Did you fall from the third floor?
EMF Detection: Blinks once: Yes.
GR Words: Texas.

Questioner: Were you from Texas?
Ghost Box: Edith.
EMF Detection: Blinks once: Yes.
Ghost Box: Houston ... Texas.

Questioner: Are you a Dallas Cowboys fan?
Observer: Please let it be two blinks.
GR Words: Duty.
Ghost Box: Falcons.
EMF Detection: Blinks twice: No.
Observers & Questioner: [*Laugh*]

Questioner: Do you like the Falcons? The Atlanta Falcons?
EMF Detection: Blinks once: Yes.
Ghost Box: Falcons.
Observer: Holy! *Wow*! That's awesome!
Ghost Box: Yep ...
EMF Detection: Blinks over thirty times.

Questioner: What does that mean? You still with me?
Ghost Box: I'm here.

Questioner: Does Matt still remind you of someone? If so, make it stop blinking.
EMF Detection: Stops blinking.
Questioner: Thank you.

Questioner: Can you tell us how old you are?
EMF Detection: Blinks twelve times.
Ghost Box: Twelve years old.

Questioner: If you are not Edith, who are you?
Ghost Box: Do not answer that.
EMF Detection: [*No response*]

Questioner: Interesting. So you are twelve years old. You're from Texas. Is that correct?
Ghost Box: Yes.
EMF Detection: Blinks once: Yes.
Ghost Box: [*Sounds like* "Edith's" or "Phoenix"]

Questioner: If you are not Edith, who are you?
Ghost Box: Edith.

Questioner: Edith, are you playing with us?
EMF Detection: Blinks twice: No.

Questioner: Is someone here with you?
Ghost Box: Bitch.
EMF Detection: Blinks once: Yes.

Questioner: Are you Edith's friend? Do you know Edith?
EMF Detection: Blinks once: Yes.
Ghost Box: Yes.

Questioner: Is Edith the one who is an angry lady?
Ghost Box: That's her, yes.
EMF Detection: Blinks once: Yes.
Ghost Box: What?
EMF Detection: Blinks twice: No.

Observers: Yes and no.
Ghost Box: I see it.

Questioner: Can you blink how many people are here?
EMF Detection: Blinks five times.

Questioner: Five? Is five correct?
Ghost Box: Five of us, right.
EMF Detection: Blinks once: Yes.
Observer: You have got to be kidding me.
Ghost Box: Fantastic.

Questioner: Can you count how many of us are here talking to you right now?
EMF Detection: Blinks eight times.
Ghost Box: Eight with us.
Observer1: There are seven of us!
Ghost Box: You.
Observer2: You forgot to count yourself; there are eight.

Questioner: So there are eight people in this room, not counting you?
Ghost Box: Yes.
EMF Detection: Blinks once: Yes.
Observer: Yes, wow.

Questioner: Do you know the guy who lives here? On this floor?
EMF Detection: [*No response*]
Ghost Box: [*No response*]

Questioner: You still here?
Ghost Box: [*two responses*] Here, yes.

EMF Detection: Blinks twice: No.
Observers: No [*laughs*], good answer.

Questioner: Do you want us to go home now?
EMF Detection: Blinks once: Yes.

Questioner: Are you tired?
EMF Detection: [*No response*]
Ghost Box: [*No response*]

Questioner: Do you consider us friends? You like us being here?
EMF Detection: Blinks three times.
Observer1: Three blinks … I don't know what that means. Maybe it's a maybe?
EMF Detection: Blinks eight times.
Observer2: It just blinked eight times.
EMF Detection: Blinks twice: No. Pauses, then blinks five times.
Observer2: I don't get it.
EMF Detection: Blinks once: Yes.

Questioner: We are going to have to go home soon. We appreciate you talking with us. Would you like us to come back and see you sometime?
EMF Detection: Blinks once: Yes.
Observer: Okay, we will come back and see you again.

Questioner: Does talking to us make you tired?
EMF Detection: Blinks once: Yes.
Observer: We apologize for wearing you out.
Ghost Box: Nice … man.

Questioner: Do you forgive us for making you tired? You mad at us?

EMF Detection: Blinks once: Yes. Pauses, then blinks twice: No.

Observer1: Yes and no. Now that's interesting. You asked two questions.

Observer2: Right, yes and no, awesome, awesome, awesome.

Questioner: Well, we are going to have to go and wrap things up now. Hopefully, we can come back and talk with you again real soon. Have a good night.

EMF Detection: Blinks many times.

End experiment.

Ghost Box Experiment: Edith and Ed

The team returned to the Ramsey Middle School investigation in Bluefield, West Virginia. We conducted a ghost box experiment in the basement of the building early in the investigation. During this experiment two spirits came through very clearly on the ghost box. One spirit, named Edith, was encountered during the first investigation. We suspected that there was a second spirit, one that was a little malevolent or maybe a trickster. During this investigation we found out that this spirit's name was Ed.

You are an angel

Dan Morgan Ramsey Middle School Investigation

Questioner [Dan]: Do you remember us from the last time we were here?
Ghost Box: Especially … yes.
Ghost Box: Witness.

Questioner [Dan]: Do you remember us from last time?
Ghost Box: Yes.

Questioner [Dan]: Would you like to talk to us?
Ghost Box: Yes.

Questioner [Dan]: This as Shawn and Dan. Can Edith hear me?
Ghost Box: Edith, Edith.
Ghost Box [clear female voice]: Need help.
Ghost Box: Too late.
Ghost Box: To heaven she went.

Questioner [Dan]: Edith has gone? Did she leave?
Ghost Box: Fourth.

Questioner [Dan]: Do you mean the fourth floor?
Ghost Box: Right.

Questioner [Dan]: Is she upstairs?
Ghost Box: Affirmative.
Ghost Box: Thank them.

Questioner [Dan]: Is Edith here?
Ghost Box: Heaven.

Questioner [Dan]: Are you saying that she left the building? Or is she high up in the building? Was Edith an angel?
Ghost Box: Hardly!
Ghost Box: Dimension.

Questioner [Dan]: Was Edith like you?
Ghost Box: Friends.

Questioner [Dan]: Sorry. We did not catch that. Was Edith like you?
Ghost Box: She can walk.
Ghost Box: Yes.

Questioner [Dan]: Did Edith belong here?
Ghost Box: Without permission.

Questioner [Dan]: Who? What is your name? Are you a ghost?
Ghost Box: We're ah spirit.
Ghost Box: In us.
Ghost Box: He comes back.
Ghost Box: Demon, has a submitter.

Questioner [Dan]: Are you the spirit of a person who lived?
Ghost Box: Yes.
Listener [Shawn]: I'm having a hard time hearing you.
Ghost Box: I know.

Listener: Try your best to come through, okay?
Ghost Box: We have come and bilaterally.

Questioner [Dan]: Who is talking?
Ghost Box: We are.

Questioner [Dan]: Tell me your name.
Ghost Box: Servant.
Ghost Box [Demanding voice]: What is your name!
Ghost Box: Edrigeah [ed-dridge-ee-ah].
Ghost Box: Ed.

Questioner [Dan]: Is your name Ed?
Ghost Box: Yes it is.

Questioner [Dan]: Where is Edith?
Ghost Box [Edith]: I'm here.

Questioner [Dan]: Edith, can you come down to the basement and talk with me?
Ghost Box: I'm listening.

Questioner [Dan]: Edith, are there angels here?
Ghost Box: Angels, yes, yes.

Questioner [Dan]: Ed, who are you?
Ghost Box: Actor.

Questioner [Dan]: Are you pretending to be something you are not?
Ghost Box: I am.

Questioner [Dan]: Edith, are you still here?
Ghost Box: Yes, kind of.
Ghost Box: Live ... person.
Ghost Box: Jesus.
Ghost Box: Heaven.

Questioner [Dan]: Are there evil spirits here?
Ghost Box: We have three of them.
Ghost Box: We need help.

Questioner [Dan]: Did you say three of them?
Ghost Box: Three.

Questioner [Dan]: Are they demons or human?
Ghost Box: Hard.

Questioner [Dan]: What? Hard?
Ghost Box: Bingo.
Ghost Box: Edith, yes.

Questioner [Dan]: Edith, were you once human? Are you still human?
Ghost Box: I am turned.
Ghost Box: Weird things.

Questioner [Dan]: [*Points to Shawn*] Do you know his name?
Ghost Box: Shawn.

Questioner [Dan]: Do you know my name?

Ghost Box: The Agent.

Observer: Mr. Smith … [*From the* Matrix *movie; snickers*]

Observer: Is he the Priest?

Ghost Box: Right, Dan.

Questioner [Dan]: But do you know what Dan is?

Ghost Box: Yes.

Ghost Box: Great … trouble.

Ghost Box: Angel.

Questioner [Dan]: Does Dan look like an angel to you?

Ghost Box: Angel.

Questioner [Dan]: Do we look like angels to you?

Ghost Box: At least.

Questioner [Dan]: At least. Do we look different?

Ghost Box: Better.

Questioner [Dan]: Are you afraid of us?

Ghost Box: You are family, you're also divine.

Ghost Box [Male voice]: I am.

Observer: We are here this time to help you.

Ghost Box [Male voice]: Who wants your help?

Observer: Especially you, Edith.

Ghost Box [Female voice]: You are an angel.

Questioner [Dan]: Edith, are you here?

Ghost Box: I can come.

Ghost Box: Time … is … short.

Questioner [Dan]: Edith, do you need help?

Ghost Box [Female voice]: Please help.

Ghost Box [Female voice]: Save me.
Ghost Box [Male voice]: Play.

Questioner [Dan]: Edith, I'm talking to you.
Ghost Box: What's the deal with this one?

Questioner [Dan]: Do you want to go to heaven?
Ghost Box: Thirsty.

Questioner [Dan]: Edith, we are going to try to help you today.
Ghost Box: Can't help us.
Ghost Box: Want … home.

Questioner [Dan]: We can help you.
Ghost Box [Male voice]: Dead.

Questioner [Dan]: If you are interacting with us, that means you still have free will to do so.
Ghost Box: Yes.

[*At this point all Edith and Ed discontinued responding to questions. They resumed communication later in the investigation.*]

End experiment.

A Message from John

In chapter 1 we briefly mention a spirit named John, who basically had the ability to break all the perceptions about ghost box limitations. Specifically, he repeatedly displayed the ability to speak entire sentences across sweep noise to make his statement. Unlike with other interactions with spirits through the box, John tends to make statements and allow you to eavesdrop on conversations he is having with other spirits, but he tends not to entertain much question-and-answer activity. In this transcription you will read how Shawn and Dan first met John, and his revelation about the years to come from that point on.

You help ghosts.

Dan Morgan (Listener in Double Blind Configuration)

Questioner [Dan]: John, are you still there?
Ghost Box [John]: I am John, from heaven.
Ghost Box [John]: God wouldn't allow evil.

Questioner [Dan]: What?
Ghost Box [John]: I warned them fourteen years
Ghost Box [John]: And
Ghost Box [John]: God dealt with them for five thousand years.
Listener: [*Jaw drop*]
Ghost Box [John]: You found them today.
Ghost Box [John]: You help ghosts.
Ghost Box [John]: Please make them believe you

Ghost Box [John]: And also find faith,
Ghost Box [John]: And I will deliver them by Christ to come into home safe.
Listener: [*Looks to be in a daze*]
Ghost Box [John]: Praise.
Ghost Box [John]: I am John, High Priest. Thank you.

Kim's Ghost Box Experiment at Ramsey Middle School

The SAI team returned to investigate at Ramsey Middle School. After Shawn and Dan obtained the message from John, Kim Payne and her team went to the basement to perform a double-blind ghost box experiment to see if they could reconnect with Edith, Ed, and John. All three came through with no problem.

Kim Payne (Questioner with EMF detector)

Questioner [Kim]: Can you touch one of us? We can't see you, but we can feel you.
Ghost Box: I can hear.

Questioner [Kim]: We can hear in these devices we are holding. Tell us what you want us to know.
Ghost Box: Wow.
Ghost Box: Ed.

Questioner [Kim]: Ed?
Ghost Box: Help.
Ghost Box: Nicolson.
Observer: Ed Nicolson.

Questioner [Kim]: Is that your last name? Make this [EMF detector] blink once for yes, twice for no.
Ghost Box: Promise?
Ghost Box: Friends.
Ghost Box: Are right here.
Ghost Box: These women.
Ghost Box: Friends.

Questioner [Kim]: Yes, all of us are friends.
Ghost Box: All?

Questioner [Kim]: How many of you are here?
Ghost Box: Three.

Questioner [Kim]: Do you know why you are still here?
Ghost Box: Punishment.
Ghost Box: For us.
Ghost Box: Space.
Ghost Box: Sin.

Ghost Box: Sin.
Ghost Box: Thanks.
Ghost Box: Both of you.
Ghost Box: Thirsty.
Ghost Box: Flame.

Questioner [Kim]: You seem very religious.
Ghost Box: Yes.

Questioner [Kim]: The last time we were here, you were talking about faith. Do you need our help?
Ghost Box: I wanta thank you.

Questioner [Kim]: Ed, if you are bothering these people, please leave them alone. Let them speak with us.
Ghost Box: Bastard.
Listener [Shelly]: Ummmmmm.
Ghost Box: Tell 'em! Enough!
Ghost Box: Monster.
Ghost Box: Ed.
Ghost Box: Poisons the ground beneath.

Questioner [Kim]: Ed, we want you to leave.
Ghost Box: Who spoke?

Questioner [Kim]: Leave now.
Ghost Box: Twenty-one

Questioner [Kim]: John, can you come talk to us?
Ghost Box [John]: Madam, work it out tonight.
Ghost Box [John]: I'll hear you.
Ghost Box: Shelly [*Listener who is holding the ghost box*], please

Ghost Box: Listen.
Ghost Box: John is beautiful.
Ghost Box: Tim.

Questioner [Kim]: You like Tim?
Observer [Tim]: There is no Tim here.
Ghost Box: Yeah.

Questioner [Kim]: Go touch him on the shoulder.
Ghost Box: Now?

Questioner [Kim]: Yes, now.
Ghost Box: Tim.
Ghost Box: Thirty [*or* "thirteen"].
Ghost Box: Handsome.

End experiment.

Shelly Taylor (Observer) and Michael Morgan (Observer)
The Ramsey Middle School investigation

Victims of the Shawnee Attack Speak

The SAI team investigated the Col. James Graham House in Lowell, West Virginia. In 1777, after the murder of Shawnee Chief Cornstalk on Mount Pleasant, the Shawnee Indian tribes began a series of raids along the American frontier. They found their way to Col. Graham House and laid siege to it, killing his ten-year-old son, John, and taking his daughter, Elizabeth, into captivity. Graham spent the next eight years searching for his daughter. The following is the transcript of the Double Blind Ghost Box experiment conducted on the two hundredth anniversary of that horrible night. The team discovered that the spirits still there at the house relive the attack over and over again.

Tim Oliver (Questioner)
Graham House investigation

Listener [Dan]: This is Shawn, Dan, and Tim in the downstairs living room of the Graham House. Ghost box session number two. Marking audio now.

Questioner1 [Shawn]: Is there anyone in this house that would like to speak to us?
Ghost Box: Here.

Questioner1 [Shawn]: Yes, we are here. In the house, in the living room by the fireplace. Can you come in here?
Ghost Box: See.

Questioner1 [Shawn]: Can you come into this room?
Ghost Box: Yes.

Questioner1 [Shawn]: Tim is holding a device. If you touch it, it will flash.
Ghost Box: Yes.

Questioner1 [Shawn]: If you come up and touch that, this is going to flash.
Ghost Box [Little girl]: Yeah.

Questioner1 [Shawn]: You can speak into the device here [*pointing to the ghost box with the ghost box recorder attached*].
Ghost Box: Better.

Questioner1 [Shawn]: Yes, we can hear you better if you use that device.

Questioner1 [Shawn]: You spoke earlier; we are now in the house, can you hear us? Can you see us?
Ghost Box: House.

Questioner1 [Shawn]: Yes, we are in the house.
Ghost Box: What part?

Questioner1 [Shawn]: We are in the old bedrooms by the fireplace on the first floor.
Ghost Box [Deep voice]: House.

Questioner1 [Shawn]: Is Elizabeth here?
Ghost Box: You got it.
Observer [Tim]: You got what?
Ghost Box: Me.

Questioner1 [Shawn]: What is your name?
Ghost Box: Me.
Ghost Box: Boy.

Questioner1 [Shawn]: Are you Elizabeth's brother?
Ghost Box: Yes.

Questioner1 [Shawn]: What is your sister's name?
Ghost Box: Liz.

Questioner2 [Tim]: What did you mean when you said you have me?
EMF Detection: Begins to blink [*debunked, caused by phone*]
Ghost Box: Hello.
Ghost Box: Who's that voice?
Ghost Box: Please.

Questioner1 [Shawn]: That is Tim.

Questioner2 [Tim]: My name is Tim. Can we help you in any way?
Ghost Box: Appreciate you being here.
Ghost Box: All of you

Questioner2 [Tim]: Can you still hear us?
Ghost Box: Go.

Questioner2 [Tim]: Where do you want us to go?
Ghost Box: Away.
Ghost Box: Free.

Questioner2 [Tim]: Why do you want us to go away? Do you not like us here?
Ghost Box: Close the door.

Questioner2 [Tim]: Which door?

Questioner1 [Shawn]: What door is open? So we can close it for you.
Ghost Box: Attic door.
[Shawn has Kim and Bryan Payne close the attic door.]
Ghost Box: Help!
Listener [Dan]: Wow ... that was clear.

Questioner2 [Tim]: You said "Help" before; what can we help you with?
Ghost Box: Please ... help ... us.

Questioner2 [Tim]: Are you being hurt?
Ghost Box: [no response]

Questioner1 [Shawn]: Do you want us to close the door in this room?
Ghost Box: Yeah.

Questioner1 [Tim closes the door]: Okay, we have closed the door.

Ghost Box: Draw the drapes.

Questioner1 [Shawn]: We can't draw the drapes.
Ghost Box: Please.

Questioner2 [Tim]: Who is outside that you do not want to look in?
Ghost Box: Drapes.
Listener [Dan]: This is not our house; we cannot draw the drapes.

Questioner1 [Shawn]: You need help cleaning up the house?
Ghost Box: Townspeople.

Questioner2 [Tim]: What is outside?
Ghost Box: "Static".
Ghost Box [Little girl's voice]: Shawnee.

Questioner1 [Shawn]: What is your name? Is it Elizabeth?
Ghost Box: Yes.

Questioner2 [Tim]: The Shawnee is outside. Is that correct?
Ghost Box: Shawnee.

Questioner2 [Tim]: Is your name Elizabeth?
Ghost Box: Dead.

Questioner2 [Tim]: You're dead? Are you saying that you are dead?
Ghost Box: I'm a spirit.
Ghost Box: Dead.

Questioner1 [Shawn]: Why are you still here? Why don't you leave?
Ghost Box: Dead.
Ghost Box: Friend listen.
Ghost Box: Dead.

Questioner2 [Tim]: How old are you? How old were you when you died?
Ghost Box: Forty.
Ghost Box: Prison camp.
Listener: What was that again?

Questioner2 [Tim]: I said, "How old were you when you died?"
Ghost Box: Forty.
Ghost Box: Ten.

Questioner2 [Tim]: Is the spirit of the Shawnee still here?
Ghost Box: Free.
Ghost Box: Free … in death.
Ghost Box: Rest.
Ghost Box: Please help them.
Ghost Box: [*crying out*] Please!
Ghost Box: Please help.
Ghost Box: Please help.

Questioner1 [Shawn]: What room were you killed in?
Ghost Box: Home.

Questioner1 [Shawn]: Were you in the kitchen?
Ghost Box: I was.

Questioner1 [Shawn]: Okay, there were only a couple people killed in that kitchen.
Ghost Box: I'm black.
Ghost Box: Stabbed me in the back.
Ghost Box: Colonel.

Observer: Colonel?
Ghost Box: Yeah.
Ghost Box: He is ... here.

Questioner2 [Tim]: Are you a colonel, sir?
Ghost Box: Yeah.
Ghost Box: I am, yeah.
Ghost Box: Right face.

Questioner1 [Shawn]: What color was your coat?
Ghost Box: Color.

Questioner1 [Shawn]: What color was your coat?
Ghost Box: Blue.
Ghost Box: Can you see it?

Questioner1 [Shawn]: Yes, we can.

End experiment.

Note: Rest assured that we did in fact come back to the Graham House and helped the spirits to rest in peace.

Multi-device Experiment at the Col. James Graham House

At the end of the night during the Col. James Graham House investigation, the team regrouped in the main living room area of the building. They set out an array of devices across a bench. This provided a wide range of options for "reported spirits" to communicate and/or to respond to inquiries from Questioners. The devices were (1) three EMF detectors, (2) a Shack Hack 12-467 ghost box, (3) an *Avatar* toy that lights up in response to touch or sound, (4) a flashlight, (5) a thermometer, and (6) an experimental smartphone application that we were looking into as a potential device for our tool kit. We will refer to that application as the "GR Words." The experiment consisted of five SAI team members; four Questioners/Observers of the experiment and one Listener with the ghost box used the double-blind method.

Dan Morgan (Listener), Bryan and Kim Payne (Questioners)
The Graham House investigation

Questioner1 [Kim]: Is there anyone here that would like to speak with us this evening?
GR Words: Couple.
Ghost Box: What happened?
GR Words: Smoke.

Questioner1 [Kim]: We smoke, me and Bryan. Did you see us smoking outside?
Ghost Box: Yes.
GR Words: Street.

Questioner1 [Kim]: We were outside by our car. What is your name?
Ghost Box: Robert.

Questioner2 [Bryan]: Robert who?
Ghost Box: Graham.

Questioner1 [Kim]: Where is Johnnie? We want to speak with Johnnie this evening. There is a toy in front of you that you can play with and make it blink [*the* Avatar *toy*].
Ghost Box: No, thanks.
GR Words: Saved.
Ghost Box: No, thank you.

Questioner2 [Bryan]: How many of us are in the room?
Ghost Box: Five.

Questioner2 [Bryan]: What color shirt does Kim have on?
Ghost Box: Steelers.
GR Words: Settlers.
Observer: What does that [*pointing to Kim's shirt*] say?
Questioner1 [Kim]: A Steelers shirt; that's close.

Questioner2 [Bryan]: How many people died in the kitchen?
Ghost Box: Three.

Questioner3 [Tim]: Is there a Walter Kellwell or a Walter Caldwell here?
Ghost Box: Yes, here.

Questioner3 [Tim]: Walt, are you in here?
Ghost Box: Behind you.

Questioner1 [Kim]: Johnnie, where is your mom? What happened to your mom?
Ghost Box: Died.

Questioner1 [Kim]: Lizzie made it okay; they found her. Did you know that? Is she with you now?
Ghost Box: [*No response*]

Questioner2 [Bryan]: John, how many brothers and sisters did you have?
Ghost Box: Elizabeth.
Ghost Box: Lizzie.

Questioner2 [Bryan]: Was she older than you?
Ghost Box: Yeah, yeah.

Questioner4 [Shawn]: Can you turn this light on over here [*pointing to a flashlight*]?
Ghost Box: [*No response*]

Questioner4 [Shawn]: Can you make this come on?
Ghost Box: Frog.
GR Words: Frog.

Questioner1 [Kim]: Yeah, I'm afraid of frogs. You must have heard me tell Dan earlier that I was not afraid of a snake in the basement but I was afraid of frogs.
Ghost Box: Graham.

Questioner5 [Dan]: Are you wanting to play a joke on Kim?
Ghost Box: Frog.

Questioner2 [Bryan]: Can you tell us what color Kim's hair is?
Ghost Box: Yellow.

Questioner4 [Shawn]: Someone says that Mr. Graham collected coins. Is that true? Did he hold money for people?
Ghost Box: [*No response*]

Questioner1 [Kim]: Is there money here, buried on the property?
Ghost Box: Yes.

Questioner4 [Shawn]: We have a wide variety of devices here that you can use to communicate with.
Ghost Box: I did.

Questioner4 [Shawn]: What room are we in right now? What do you call this room?
Ghost Box: Home.

Questioner4 [Shawn]: There is only one object that came from this original family. [*Shawn picks up a hackle*]. It's basically a board with nails through it. They would use it to rake across wool for the weaving wheel. Like a type of brush.

Questioner1 [Kim]: Did you use that instrument? Did you have to help with the wool?
Ghost Box: Keep.

Questioner5 [Dan]: [*Dan picks up the hackle.*] Do you like me holding this?
Ghost Box: Dan.

Questioner3 [Tim]: They were the first ones to make holes in jeans. They started it. What's it called again?
Ghost Box: Hackle.

Questioner4 [Shawn]: What do you call this place?
Ghost Box: Safe.

Questioner1 [Kim]: Can you say that again? What do you call this place?
Ghost Box: Safe.

Questioner4 [Shawn]: Can you take energy out of the air and make it colder?
Ghost Box: Yes.
[*Tim takes the headset and becomes the Listener.*]

Questioner2 [Bryan]: Who has the headphones on now?
Ghost Box: Tim!

Questioner1 [Kim]: Okay, it is sixty-five degrees; drop it three more degrees.
Ghost Box: Dan.
Ghost Box: Save us.

Questioner5 [Dan]: Hello?

Ghost Box: Help me.

Questioner2 [Bryan]: Was Sharp a slave?
Ghost Box: Yes.

Questioner4 [Shawn]: Where did we see Sharp? Where is that coming from?
Ghost Box: Music.
Questioner5 [Dan]: Sharp was the one that got killed in the kitchen.
Ghost Box: Dan has it.
GR Words: Best.

Questioner1 [Kim]: Was he the best slave that you had here? He took care of you, didn't he?
GR Words: Treated.
Questioner1 [Kim]: That was very nice of him. He tried to protect you when the Indians got here.

Questioner2 [Bryan]: Can you tell us what your last name is?
Ghost Box: Grimes.
Ghost Box [Deep, demanding male voice]: No.

Questioner2 [Bryan]: Are you in trouble?
Ghost Box: Yes.
Ghost Box: Yes.
[EMF Detector 1 starts blinking all of a sudden. There were no responses on any of the three EMF detectors up to this point.]
Observer: Okay, that's interesting.

Questioner1 [Kim]: What can we help you with?
GR Words: Weather.
Ghost Box: Weapons.

Ghost Box: Promise.

[EMF Detector 1 starts blinking again.]

Observer: What is going on? Why is that going off all of a sudden?

Listener [Tim]: I think this is a phone. I can hear it in the ghost box.

Ghost Box: Message.

Observer: How do you know it's a phone?

GR Words: Information.

Observer: What the heck?

Observer: It's not a phone. We need to figure out what is going on here.

Observer: We have the phones here, and none of them are ringing.

Observer: Tim, how do you know this is a phone?

Listener [Tim]: I can hear the signal, like a text message coming through. Like that pop, pop, pop, pop sound you hear when a text is coming in.

Observer: I know what you are talking about.

Observer: This is the thing, when we were outside we noticed that the ghost box and EMF detector are linked. As that was detecting EMF spikes, you could hear whatever was going on through the ghost box.

Listener [Tim]: When I started to hear that popping sound, that is when the EMF started going off. It sounds just like cell phone frequencies.

EMF Detector1: Blinks once.

Questioner4 [Shawn]: Okay, how about this? If that is an entity that is touching that, can you do it right now?

EMF Detectors1&2: Start blinking.

Ghost Box: [*The sound of interference, like a data transmission buzz, is heard.*]

Questioner4 [Shawn]: Can you do it again right now?
EMF Detectors1&2: Blink for a few seconds.
Ghost Box: [*The sound of interference, like a data transmission buzz, is heard again.*]
GR Words: Meant.
Observer [Dan]: Meant? Interesting.

Questioner1 [Kim]: You meant to do that?
Ghost Box: Dan.
Listener [Tim]: I can hear the sound in the ghost box just a moment before we see it on the EMF detectors.
Ghost Box: Dan.
Observer [Shawn]: Okay, that's good.

Questioner5 [Dan]: Can you blink them once for yes, twice for no?
Ghost Box: Listen.
Ghost Box: Please.

Questioner5 [Dan]: Can you blink them once for yes, twice for no?
Ghost Box: Interference.

Questioner4 [Shawn]: Okay, how about this? If this is you, and you have the ability to move around, can you make the one [EMF detector 3] by Kim go off?
Ghost Box: Hundred.
GR Words: Vertical.
Ghost Box: Touch.

Questioner4 [Shawn]: Okay, Kim, can you turn that EMF detector so it's pointing up and down vertically? [*Kim repositions EMF detector.*]
Ghost Box: Close.
Ghost Box: Hi.

Questioner4 [Shawn]: Can you rub the one, by Kim?
Ghost Box: So cute.
Ghost Box: One.

Questioner2 [Bryan]: What were you needing us to help you with?
Ghost Box: This.
Observer: You definitely got our attention.
Ghost Box: Thank you.

Questioner1 [Kim]: Who is with us now?
Ghost Box: [*unknown response, sounds like "blood"*]
Observer: I think he has found his groove [*referring to Tim on the ghost box using the double-blind process*].
Ghost Box: Yes.

Questioner4 [Shawn]: Can you touch those orange lights again [*pointing to the three EMF detectors*]?
Ghost Box: Listen … three.
Ghost Box: Three.

Questioner4 [Shawn]: On one, two, three, now.
GR Words: Car.
Ghost Box: Car.
[*Just as a car passes the house in the middle of the night*]
Observer: A car just went by.
Ghost Box: Yes.

Questioner4 [Shawn]: Okay, I want you to touch the detectors with the orange lights on them that you touched earlier and made blink. Can you do it again on one, two, three, now?
Ghost Box: I missed it.
Ghost Box: [*Produces the sound of interference, like a data transmission*]
[*No reaction from the EMF detectors*]
Observer: That was really weird; it was quiet all night, then all of a sudden everything just lit up like a Christmas tree in here.
Listener [Tim]: They sound so far away.
Observer: It's odd, because even though it seems like the phones are causing it, they are responding to questions.
Observer: We are seeing a pattern here where it's a lot of activity, then all of a sudden dead.

Questioner1 [Kim]: Does it take you time to get enough energy to talk to us?
Ghost Box: Temperature.
Observer [Shawn]: What is the temperature at now?
Observer [Bryan]: 66.8 degrees. I thought it was getting colder.
Listener [Tim]: You know what was weird earlier? I heard, like, a whisper, not like a digital whisper, but like voices in the background cutting across.
Observer [Shawn]: Yeah, we experienced the same thing. It's like you can hear the radio. That part is going, but underneath it is a whisper; but it is so far away.
Listener [Tim]: It's definitely not digital, I know that.
Observer [Shawn]: It's so hard to hear, though.
Listener [Tim]: They are.

Questioner1 [Kim]: We were asking earlier: who was the president when you were alive [*referring to 1777*]?
Ghost Box: Didn't have a president.
Ghost Box: Challenge.

[*Dan gets the idea to send a text from his phone to one of the phones directly beside an EMF detector. The EMF detectors do not respond, and the ghost box does not hear the outgoing or incoming data frequency.*]
GR Words: Opinion.
Ghost Box: What's that do?
Observer [Shawn]: So the text did not set off anything.
Ghost Box: No.
Ghost Box [Male voice]: Drop it, it's no coincidence.
Ghost Box: Right.
Ghost Box: [*Yells*] Right!

End experiment.

As a result of this experiment, from then on the SAI team turns all phones to airplane mode during investigations. It was notable that the EMF detectors seemed to be responding to questions with perfect timing in conjunction with the ghost box and GR Words application. However, it is inconclusive evidence that spirits were manipulating the frequencies to cause the EMF detectors to trigger or not trigger when cell frequencies were present. It was apparent during evidence review that the EMF detectors went off only when the ghost box heard the cell frequencies. However, there were also times when the frequencies could be heard but did not trigger the EMF detectors. The evidence here shows that the ghost box was dependable in its ability to detect the cell phone interference, which may help debunk free-roaming radio frequencies in a location. It also clearly produced relevant responses to questions that the Listener could not hear and was able to answer even trick questions such as who was the president at that time. As mentioned before in this book, many times we go to a location asking specific questions about events that happened during the lives of "reported spirits'" only to get responses about events not in the expected time frame. This was not the case at the Col. James Graham House. The responses could be accurately dated back to the target time period with no interference from overlapping levels of time.

The Turning Point: George Pearis Cemetery

The historic Pearis Cemetery is located at the western edge of Pearisburg, Virginia, in the area sometimes called Bluff City. For years it was overgrown, neglected, and mostly forgotten. But several years ago the Town of Pearisburg (with the help of several other organizations) restored it. The cemetery includes the grave of Captain George Pearis, for whom the town is named. He fought in the Revolutionary War. The SAI team was called in to investigate claims of paranormal activity. The following is the transcript of two double-blind experiments performed by the team during the investigation.

*Dan Morgan, Amy Buchanan, and David Henderson (Questioners)
The Pearis Cemetery Investigation*

Questioner1 [Dan]: All right, if you want help, we need to know why you need help.

Ghost Box: Odin.

Observer1 [Amy]: Odin?

Ghost Box: David.

Observer1 [Amy]: That's weird.

Observer2 [Dave]: Not to throw you guys off here, but I am wearing an Odin necklace.

Observer1 [Amy]: Um, Dan, Dave is wearing an Odin necklace.

Observer3 [Dan]: Wow.

[*Amy gets Shawn's, the Listener's, attention*]

Observer1 [Amy]: Hey, Dave's wearing an Odin necklace.

Observer4 [Shawn]: You are kidding me.

Observer2 [Dave]: No, man, it was just under my shirt so you couldn't see it.

Observer4 [Shawn]: Okay, that's interesting.

[Shawn puts the headphones back on and continues as the Listener in the Double Blind Ghost Box configuration.]
Observer3 [Dan]: Okay, you got our attention.
Ghost Box: Focus.
Listener [Shawn]: That sounded like John giving instructions. I think that was John.

Questioner2 [Amy]: Well, is John here?
GB Words 1 [Amy's Device]: Victory.
Observer3 [Dan]: Interesting.
GB Words 2 [Dan's Device]: Success.
Observer3 [Dan]: Are you kidding me?
GB Words 3 [Dave's Device]: Cast.

Questioner1 [Dan]: Can you tell us why you are still here? Some of you say you realize you are dead. Some of you are saying you are trapped, while others say you're not.
Ghost Box: Here it comes.
[A train blows its horn very loud just after the ghost box says, "Here it comes."]
Observer1 [Amy]: Yep, the train!
Observer3 [Dan]: Wow! Are you kidding?
GB Words 1 [Amy's Device]: Ride.
Observer4 [Shawn]: That's what I'm talking about, that was killer. Awesome!

Questioner1 [Dan]: Can you tell us why you are here? Do you know why you are here?
Ghost Box: I am dead.

Questioner1 [Dan]: Okay, we get that, but why are you still here and not on the other side?
Ghost Box: Ten.

Ghost Box: Ten thousand.

Listener [Shawn]: Odd. It is just saying "ten thousand" over and over.

Ghost Box: Ten.

Ghost Box: Thousand.

Listener [Shawn]: They are just repeating it over and over again. They are going crazy over that number. I don't get it.

Ghost Box: Ten thousand.

GB Words 2 [Dan's device]: Later.

Ghost Box: Ten thousand.

Listener [Shawn]: Again, again, ten thousand. Okay, we got it, we hear you. Now help us understand what it is you are trying to say here.

Questioner1 [Dan]: Okay, what about ten thousand?

Ghost Box: Go home.

Ghost Box: In.

Ghost Box: Ten thousand.

Questioner3 [Dave]: Are they bound here for ten thousand years?

Ghost Box: Ten thousand.

End experiment.

The team ended the ghost box experiment in order to conduct other experiments outside the scope of this book. They returned at the end of the night to conduct the final experiment and to follow up on information gathered so far. It is apparent up to this point that the spirits at the George Pearis Cemetery needed help crossing over. They were led to believe that after ten thousand years they would be allowed to cross over and go home. The team planned to get to the bottom of this delusion and help them cross over now. What you are about to read was *the turning point* in SAI history!

Listener [Shawn]: This is ghost box session number two. George Pearis Cemetery. Mark audio.

GB Words 2 [Dan's device]: Experiment.

[A train blows its horn very loud just after the listener repeats the word "experiment."]

Observer4 [Shawn]: Did that just happen? Okay, talk about timing, wow.

Questioner1 [Dan]: So, we are back. Do you have anything new to say? Or would you like to talk more about help?

Ghost Box: Desperate.

Questioner1 [Dan]: Desperate for help or what?

Ghost Box: Help us.

Ghost Box: Poison.

Ghost Box: In all of us.

Ghost Box: Need help.

GB Words 2 [Dan's device]: Gate.

Ghost Box: Home.

Questioner1 [Dan]: Do you want to go home? Is there someone here oppressing everyone else? Keeping everyone else down? Is there an evil boss here?

Ghost Box: Here.

Ghost Box: In us.

Ghost Box: Horseman.

Ghost Box: Demon.

Ghost Box: He gave us.

Ghost Box: Evil.

Ghost Box: Evil each.

Ghost Box: Evil each in us.
Ghost Box: From?
Ghost Box: During.
Ghost Box: Ten thousand.
GB Words 1 [Amy's device]: Against.

Questioner1 [Dan]: Can you call on the name of Jesus?
Ghost Box: Of course.

Questioner1 [Dan]: Can you do it now?
Listener [Shawn]: It sounded like they all just backed away. It just changed. It's like, um, there was a bunch of voices that were talking, and I could understand the repetition of who they were. It's like you have five people there, and they are talking to you. Then all five of them just disappeared. They are not there anymore.

Questioner1 [Dan]: Is anybody left with us here? Is there anybody here with us now? At all?
Ghost Box: He is.
Ghost Box: Now.

Questioner1 [Dan]: Who is?
Ghost Box: Help!
Ghost Box: [*Sounds like* Be-A-Zil]
Ghost Box: Be-A-Zil.
Listener [Shawn]: They said it twice.
Ghost Box: Be-A-Zil.
Listener [Shawn]: Three times.
Observer3 [Dan]: Hmm, that's what I'm looking for.

Questioner4/Listener [Shawn]: What are you trying to say?
Ghost Box: Be-A-Zil.

Listener [Shawn]: It's like it is saying "Bezil" or "Bal."

Observer3 [Dan]: What?

Ghost Box: Please listen.

[Dan gets Shawn's attention and inquires, "You can't understand it? It's a name that you could not pronounce?"]

Listener [Shawn]: It's a name. It sounds like Bazel.

GB Words 1 [Amy's device]: German.

Observer3 [Dan]: German?

Listener [Shawn]: Something like Be-A-Zil or something

Ghost Box: Correct!

Listener [Shawn]: Wo, wo, they said correct! When I said "Be-A-Zil," they said, "Correct."

Questioner1 [Dan]: Are you a demon? Is Be-A-Zil a demon?

Ghost Box: Yes.

Ghost Box: Demon.

Questioner1 [Dan]: What is your business here?

Ghost Box [Deep male voice]: WALK!

Observer1 [Amy]: Walk?

[The team then hears in the distance something yell, "WALK!"]

Observer1 [Amy]: What was that?

Observer3 [Dan]: Did you hear that?

Observer3 [Dan]: Did you flippin' hear that?

Observer2 [Dave]: Yeah.

Observer1 [Amy]: What in the world?

[Dan gets Shawn's attention.]

Observer3 [Dan]: We just heard somebody say "WALK!"

Observer1 [Amy]: Yeah.

Observer3 [Dan]: From over there [*pointing to the distant mountains by the cemetery*].

Observer1 [Amy]: From over there.

Observer4 [Shawn]: Yeah?

111

Observer3 [Dan]: Something goes, "W<small>ALK</small>!"

Observer4 [Shawn]: Yeah, that's what it did in here [*pointing to the ghost box*].

Observer3 [Dan]: We all heard it out here, over that way.

Observer4 [Shawn]: Yeah, so we may have something here [*referring to external events corresponding to things heard on the ghost box*].

Observer3 [Dan]: Yeah.

Observer4 [Shawn]: Interesting.

Observer4 [Shawn]: See, this is one of the reasons why you never know what you are going to run into on an investigation [*referring specifically to demons*].

Observer3 [Dan]: I sure hope our recorders picked that up.

Observer4 [Shawn]: So right now, in the name of Jesus, I protect this team by your blood. Set your angels around us.

Ghost Box: And around us.

[*Fast rustling sound in the trees around the team*]

Observer1 [Amy]: What was that?

Observer3 [Dan]: I don't know.

Observer3 [Dan]: Really?

Observer4/Listener [Shawn]: Yeah, that's what they just said: "And around us" when I said that.

Observer1 [Amy]: Something was over that way.

Observer3 [Dan]: Yeah, I heard it too.

Observer1 [Amy]: It was something was over that way. I don't know what it was.

Observer3 [Dan]: I don't either.

Ghost Box: The demon is going.

Ghost Box: He's frozen.

Questioner1 [Dan]: Can you answer us now?

Ghost Box: Imprisoned.

Questioner1 [Dan]: But you can be released.

Ghost Box: Demon come.

[*The wind all of a sudden picks up and begins to rattle the flagpole just over the heads of the team. The flag catches a random gust of wind, which whips it all over the place.*]

Observer3 [Dan]: What the heck ...

Observer2 [Dave]: Oh my God.

Observer3 [Dan]: ... is the flag doing!

Questioner1 [Dan]: Talk to us.

Listener [Shawn]: They are on that ten-thousand thing again, just repeating it over and over.

Ghost Box [John]: I lost them.

Listener [Shawn]: Um, that was John! He said "I lost them."

Listener [Shawn]: They were saying the ten-thousand thing, and John jumps in and goes "I lost them." Like he got frustrated. It's the same voice.

Questioner1 [Dan]: John, is there something we can do at this point [to help them]?

Ghost Box [John]: Bishops, bring it.

Ghost Box [John]: Here.

Questioner2 [Amy]: What do you want us to bring?

Ghost Box [John]: Miracle.

Ghost Box [Woman's voice]: Demon, get out.

Listener [Shawn]: I think someone is trying to fight back against the demon.

Observer3 [Dan]: I second that.

Ghost Box: He is comfortable.

Observer3 [Dan]: I don't care if he is comfortable or not.

Observer1 [Amy]: He can just go on.

Observer3 [Dan]: I come against you! I command you to leave and let these people go. Go far away from here, NOW!

Ghost Box: Now

Ghost Box [John]: God come.

Observer4/Listener [Shawn]: I agree [with John's statement].

Observer4 [Shawn]: God, save these people. I don't know what to do. All I can do is be here [for them].

Ghost Box [Deep male voice]: You request.

Observer4 [Shawn]: I bind up this demon and cast it away.

Ghost Box [Demon]: Host!

Ghost Box [Demon]: Host!

Ghost Box [Demon]: HOST!

Ghost Box: Be-A-Zil

Observer4/Listener [Shawn]: YOU CANNOT TAKE ANYONE! YOU LEAVE NOW! YOU ARE NOT TO STEP ON THIS LAND ANY MORE! YOU CANNOT HAVE A HOST!

Ghost Box: Get your hands off of him!

Observer3 [Dan]: That was interesting.

Listener [Shawn]: There is a struggle going on. I can hear it. It's weird.

Observer3 [Dan]: Really? Mark that.

Listener [Shawn]: There is something going on.

Ghost Box: Help.

Ghost Box: Bible.

Observer1 [Amy]: Wow.

GB Words 2 [Dan's device]: School.

Ghost Box: Fascinating.

Ghost Box: Angel.

Ghost Box: Christ.

Ghost Box: Angel.

Listener [Shawn]: It's almost like there is something going on …

Ghost Box: Your angel covers.

Listener [Shawn]: ... And then there is bystanders.

Ghost Box: Be-A-Zil.

Listener [Shawn]: And there is cheerleaders that are going "Awesome."

Ghost Box: Priest.

Listener [Shawn]: ...and they are saying, like, really cool stuff. It's really weird. I'm seeing, like, this whole thing in here [*pointing to the ghost box*].

Ghost Box: It is happening.

Ghost Box: Affirmative.

Listener [Shawn]: That's a weird word, "affirmative."

Observer1 [Amy]: It's like military.

Observer3 [Dan]: We have heard that before, though.

Ghost Box: [*Trumpet sound*]

Ghost Box [John]: I have opened it.

Listener [Shawn]: That was John.

Observer3 [Dan]: Good.

Observer4 [Shawn]: I can't believe it. This is, like, the first time we are actually seeing progress being made [*referring to helping spirits*].

Observer3 [Dan]: Yeah.

Observer1 [Amy]: Yeah, they are fighting evil.

Ghost Box [John]: Jesus.

Listener [Shawn]: I'm hearing cool sounds, strange sounds, different sounds [*like rushing of wind and water and lightning*].

Observer3 [Dan]: Interesting.

[*Dan's battery in his camera dies.*]

Observer3 [Dan]: That was weird [*not knowing why the camera just turned off*].

Listener [Shawn]: They are all starting to quiet down.

Observer3 [Dan]: Oh, my battery just died!
Ghost Box [John]: Shalom.
Observer3 [Dan]: Shalom [*in response to John*].
Observer1 [Amy]: Shalom?

At this point another spirit joins John and addresses the group of other spirits from the cemetery. We do not know his name so we will just call him Joshua so that you can follow his words.

Ghost Box [Joshua]: I'm here.
Listener [Shawn]: Oh my.
Ghost Box [Joshua]: Water.
Ghost Box [Joshua]: Is.
Ghost Box [Joshua]: Expired.
Ghost Box [Joshua]: I will give you rest.
Listener [Shawn]: Oh my God, Dan.
Observer3 [Dan]: [*Smiles*] I can't wait to hear it!
Ghost Box [Joshua]: Remember.
Ghost Box [Joshua]: Christ.
Ghost Box: Praise the blood.
Ghost Box [Joshua]: Join us.
Listener [Shawn]: They are leaving!
Observer3 [Dan]: You are kidding.
Listener [Shawn]: They are leaving. I'm hearing less and less voices; they stopped talking.
Ghost Box: You found us.
Listener [Shawn]: They are all moving away like …
Ghost Box: Spirit.
Listener [Shawn]: It's getting …
Ghost Box: Help us.
Listener [Shawn]: The voices, there are fewer and fewer.
Observer3 [Dan]: Like someone is walking off.
Listener [Shawn]: Like they are all going away …

Ghost Box [Joshua]: Take rest in me.
Ghost Box: Rest.
Listener [Shawn]: I'm hearing like they are floating away.
Ghost Box: Free us from here.
Ghost Box [Joshua]: Rest.
Observer3 [Dan]: That's going to be one of the most interesting ghost box audios ever.
Ghost Box: I'm coming, heaven!
Listener [Shawn]: I can't believe this is happening.
Listener [Shawn]: Amen.
Ghost Box: Jesus.
Observer3 [Dan]: So be it.
Ghost Box: Jesus.
Listener [Shawn]: There might be a couple left.
Observer3 [Dan]: By choice.
Ghost Box [John]: The end is here.
Ghost Box [John]: Believe it.

End experiment.

[*John 5:28: Do not be amazed at this, for a time is coming when all who are in their graves will hear His voice and come out ...*]

The Bluewell Case

This was a case in which two houses were built on a plot of land in Bluewell West Virginia in the 1930s. The grandmother of the client passed away in 2007, while living in one of the houses. Two years later the grandmother's house mysteriously burned to the ground. Witnesses at the time saw what looked like a giant burning cross in the flames. Allegedly, a man hanged himself in the grandmother's house; then, a year later, a young child and mother were murdered there. The client and her family have lived in the adjacent house for twelve years. The previous owners practiced satanic rituals in the basement, leaving what looked like bloodstains on the floor, and symbols all over the walls. The claims about the remaining house included moving objects, shadow figures, mimics, and aggression toward men and the client's baby daughter.

The SAI team was called in to investigate the haunting and to remove the spirits tormenting the family. The following is the transcript from the ghost box experiment conducted at the end of the investigation. The efforts were to uncover why these spirits were here, why they wanted to bring harm to the baby, and how the fire started at the first house, and to give instructions for the spirits to leave the home in peace.

Tim Oliver (Observer) and David Henderson (Listener)
The Bluewell Case

Questioner1 [Dan]: This is Dan, Shawn, Tim, Amy, and David. Ghost box session, Bluewell Case. Mark audio.

Questioner1 [Dan]: We have a device here that will allow us to hear you in real time. Can you tell us what your name is?
Ghost Box: Clear.

Questioner1 [Dan]: Can you tell us your name?
Ghost Box: Donald. [*Note: This was the name of the home owner that built the houses in the thirties.*]

Questioner1 [Dan]: Why are you here?
[*Unknown sound heard in the room, like a growling sound*]
Observer1 [Dan]: What was that?
Observer2 [Amy]: I don't know.
Observer3 [Dave]: I heard it too.
Observer1 [Dan]: That was really weird.
[*The team marks audio for evidence review.*]
Observers 1, 2 & 3: Mark.
Ghost Box: Dark.
Ghost Box: Sugar.

Questioner1 [Dan]: Was that you that just talked to us?
Ghost Box: Yes.

Questioner1 [Dan]: Is Salina here? [*Donald's daughter, Salina, and his wife were killed in a car accident.*]
Ghost Box: Yes, here.
Ghost Box: Dan.

Questioner1 [Dan]: Can I help you? Is there something I can do for you?
Ghost Box: Save him.
Ghost Box: Donald.

Questioner1 [Dan]: Are you having a hard time communicating?

Ghost Box: Too clear ... help.

Questioner2 [Tim]: Salina, you here, sugar? [*Donald referenced Salina by "sugar" in letters.*]
Ghost Box [Young girl's voice]: Too many.

Questioner1 [Dan]: Too many what?
Ghost Box [Young girl's voice]: Sounds.
Ghost Box [Young girl's voice]: These are enough.

Questioner1 [Dan]: We need to know what to do to help you.
Ghost Box: Deal with them.
Ghost Box: Priest.
Ghost Box: Escaped.
Ghost Box: Renounce them.
Observer1 [Dan]: I renounce evil spirits in this place.
Ghost Box: Let's have their names.
Observer1 [Dan]: I bind them.
Observer1 [Dan]: I renounce any evil spirits.
Ghost Box: Nine.

Questioner1 [Dan]: I command any spirits who would be against these, who want peace, to leave. Is there anyone here who wants to leave?
Ghost Box: Everyone.
Ghost Box: There.
Ghost Box: Save them.
Ghost Box: Do it.
Ghost Box: Please.

Questioner1 [Dan]: I bind all evil spirits here. I renounce any spell that was ever cast; any summoning ever done here. I cast any evil spirit, any nonhuman entity into the dry place.

Ghost Box: I hope not.

Questioner1 [Dan]: You do not have a right to be here. You do not have a right over these souls.
Questioner1 [Dan]: Does anyone see a light?
Ghost Box: No.
Ghost Box: No.

Questioner1 [Dan]: A gate? A door?
Ghost Box: Gate.

Questioner1 [Dan]: Flee to it. Run to it as hard as you can.
Ghost Box: Gate.

[*The SAI team takes a break, then returns with Dave as the Listener.*]

Questioner1 [Dan]: So we are back to the question: "What is your name?"
Ghost Box: Priest [*referring to Dan*].

Questioner1 [Dan]: Yes?
Ghost Box: The great men travel with Christ.
Ghost Box: Priest.

Questioner2 [Shawn]: Can you hear me?
Ghost Box: Sir.

Questioner2 [Shawn]: How many people are in this room right here?
Ghost Box: Five people.

[*The ghost box stopped answering questions for a while.*]

Questioner1 [Dan]: Listen, we will focus if you will talk, but you have got to answer questions.
Ghost Box: I'm trying.

Questioner1 [Dan]: Tell me your name.
Ghost Box: Name.
Ghost Box: Rachel is there. [*This is the name of the client's grandmother that passed away in the house.*]

Questioner1 [Dan]: Do you dislike the baby?
Ghost Box: [*No response*]

Questioner1 [Dan]: Do you want to get rid of the baby?
Ghost Box: I said, I love you.
Listener2 [Dave] [misheard the box and said]: "*He* said, *he* loves you."
Ghost Box [corrects Dave, saying]: "*I* said."

Questioner2 [Shawn]: Does it make you angry if we pack everything up in this house and move out?
Ghost Box: Yes.
Ghost Box: Help.
Ghost Box: Fire.
Observer1 [Dan]: It's interesting with the house fire next door.

Questioner1 [Dan]: Did you start the fire?
Ghost Box: Got in somehow.
Ghost Box: Inside the room.
Ghost Box: Someone breaks in house.
Ghost Box: Please find out.

Questioner2 [Shawn]: Where do you live?

Ghost Box: Our house is empty.

Questioner1 [Dan]: We only have a couple more minutes. So make this good.
Questioner2 [Shawn]: Do you have a message for this family? This is not about you. It is not about the fire. This is about the people who live here in this house. Do you have a message for them? Is there anything specific that you need to tell them?
Ghost Box: Warning.

Questioner2 [Shawn]: Is this house going to catch on fire?
Ghost Box: Later.
Ghost Box: They're dead.

Questioner1 [Dan]: They need to move on.
Ghost Box: Waiting.

Questioner1 [Dan]: For what?
Ghost Box: For you.

Questioner1 [Dan]: For me to what?
Ghost Box: To leave.
Ghost Box: Found us.
Ghost Box: Someplace safer.
Ghost Box: Elsewhere.
Ghost Box: We found them.
Ghost Box: Dead.
Ghost Box: Us.
Ghost Box: Find us.
Ghost Box: Homeless.

Questioner1 [Dan]: By the authority of Jesus Christ I bless this house.

Ghost Box: Push.

Questioner1 [Dan]: We command any evil spirits to leave. We renounce any dominion that may have been given. If you a malevolent spirit …
Ghost Box: Malevolent.
Questioner1 [Dan]: … We tell you to move on.
Ghost Box: Someone invited them here.

Questioner1 [Dan]: It is time to leave this house alone, this family alone.
Ghost Box: If you can fight them.
Questioner1 [Dan]: I do not have to.

Questioner2 [Shawn]: So, you were you invited in?
Ghost Box: Can't stop me.
Ghost Box: They allowed us.

Questioner1 [Dan]: So, Lord, we bless this house. We pray that you would protect the family. We pray that you would protect the home. We pray that you would protect the people coming in and out of this home. Lord, we understand the authority we have, and so we tell these spirits to leave.
Ghost Box: Fight you.

Questioner2 [Shawn]: In the name of Jesus we bind up every door, every gateway into this home. In the name of Jesus Christ, whatever spirit is here that comes against this family in any way must leave NOW, in the name of Jesus. You are not welcome here. You must go …
Ghost Box: Don't do it, stop.
Ghost Box: Stop!

Questioner2 [Shawn]: Now! You must leave! This is not a debate. You are leaving now.

Questioner1 [Dan]: The ones who summoned you are not here. You are no longer welcome.

Questioner2 [Shawn]: Lord, when we are gone, set up angels here to protect this property. The people who live here may not know how to sustain these walls.
Ghost Box: Pull it down.

Questioner2 [Shawn]: Lord, we ask that you sustain these walls for us, for them.

Questioner1 [Dan]: Thank you, Lord, for your victory.

Questioner2 [Shawn]: Amen.

Questioner2 [Shawn]: Amen.
Ghost Box: Priest Quit!

Questioner2 [Shawn]: Amen.

Questioner3 [Tim]: Father, I know that you will put a hedge of protection around this house. I pray for this family that you show them your power.
Ghost Box: Hope.

Questioner3 [Tim]: And that you show them that there is hope in you, God. There always has been. We thank you for this opportunity, God. Just show your love and your power. We know that your angels are here. The demons have no business being here. They have to leave. They have to go. That is all there is to it.

Listener2 [Dave]: I just caught a bunch of them say, "Later."

Observers [Shawn & Dan]: Good.

Observer1 [Dan]: Yeah, I don't think they like it.

Questioner2 [Shawn]: Let your peace be on this house. Allow your spirit to fill it. We have planted the seeds in a dark place. Where your Spirit is, there is a spirit of freedom. Surround this place by your power and your love, Lord. Amen

Ghost Box: [no more responses]

End experiment.

Mountain Lake Hotel

The Ballroom Ghost Box experiment at the Mountain Lake Hotel was similar to the events at the George Pearis Cemetery. We were able to observe external events that linked directly back to ghost box activities as they unfolded. In the ballroom John ministers to spirits, quoting Psalm 28, and explains to them that "the sacrifice, Jesus, has risen." A group of spirits believed the message of Christ and crossed over with John. Afterward, witnesses of the event, specifically one in particular, openly rejected the message. They were confused about why and how the group left, even though it happened right in front of them. This was truly an amazing observation. We begin with Amy, Dave, and Amanda in the library, just outside of the main lobby at the hotel.

David Henderson (Listener)
Mountain Lake Hotel and Resort Investigation

Listener [Dave]: This box is going to create a bunch of static. It should give you a little something you can use to communicate with. It will give you a little bit of background noise to pull from.

Questioner1 [Amy]: Is there anyone here who would like to speak with us?
Ghost Box: Me.

Questioner1 [Amy]: Miss Moody, are you here with us?
Ghost Box: No.

Questioner1 [Amy]: Is the little redheaded boy here with us?
Ghost Box: Closer.

Listener [Dave]: I'm hearing some voices but I haven't gotten into the groove yet. There is, however, a deep man's voice. Like, I mean, a really deep. Like Bubba Smith, *Police Academy*, deep. So all right … back to it.

Questioner1 [Amy]: If you are the gentleman that Dave is talking about, can you give us a name?
Ghost Box: Several.
Listener [Dave]: That was a female, by the way.

Questioner1 [Amy]: You have several names?
Ghost Box: Yes.
Ghost Box: Asshole.
Listener [Dave]: Dude, there is some seriously verbal stuff going on right now.
Observer1 [Amanda]: [*Gets Dave's attention*]: Like cussing?
Listener [Dave]: Yeah.
Observer1 [Amanda]: All righty, then.

Questioner2 [Amanda]: So, since we don't want you to repeat that, can you say something a little less vulgar?
Ghost Box: I said that.
Ghost Box: Are you kidding?

Questioner1 [Amy]: Who is the guy saying all these vulgar things? Tell me your name.
Ghost Box: Terrible.

Questioner2 [Amanda]: Who … are … we … talking … to?
Ghost Box: [*Mocking Amanda's tone*] I … don't … know.
Ghost Box: Bring it!
[*Amy shrieks "Ow!"; got the dickens shocked out of her while turning on a light.*]
Observer2 [Dave]: Careful, did you get shocked?
Observer3 [Amy]: Yeah, that hurt!
Listener/Observer2 [Dave]: Mark audio two.

Questioner1 [Amy]: If that was somebody who shocked me, can you give me a name?
Ghost Box: William.

Questioner1 [Amy]: William, what is your last name?
Ghost Box: Last name?
Listener [Dave]: It sounds like someone is fighting right now. You can hear, like, the people hitting each other, fists hitting, pounding.
Ghost Box: [*Extreme yell*]
Listener [Dave]: WOAH! It just sounds like someone got the tar beat out of them. They yelped. Like someone hit something and got hurt.

Shawn Taylor (Listener)
Mountain Lake Hotel and Resort Investigation

[*Meanwhile, Shawn and Dan are downstairs in the dining area conducting an EVP session.*]

Questioner [Shawn]: A friend of mine earlier told you to go up into the attic and grab my pants leg; you did that. Can you

return the favor? Can you go run up to him and grab his pants leg? Do to him the same thing you did to me.
Listener [Dave]: Shawn.

Questioner2 [Amanda]: What about Shawn?
Ghost Box: I will move him.
[*Amy and Amanda hear an audible growling sound in the room.*]
Listener [Dave]: I felt my pants leg move.
Observer1 [Amanda]: Uh, we just heard a growl.
Observer3 [Amy]: We just heard a growl.
Ghost Box: Wake up!

Questioner1 [Amy]: Is there anything we can do [to help you]?
Ghost Box: Break free.
Listener [Dave]: That was loud and clear.
Ghost Box: Thank you.

Questioner1 [Amy]: You know, we are here to help you.
Ghost Box: A marvel

Questioner1 [Amy]: We are here to help you cross over if you want. To go into heaven.
Ghost Box: He wants.
Ghost Box: A higher up.
Ghost Box: Where is the preacher?
Observer3 [Amy]: Down the hall.
Ghost Box: That's correct.
Ghost Box: Get him.
Ghost Box: Being fruitful

Questioner1 [Amy]: John, are you here?
Ghost Box: John is with the others.

Ghost Box: The group.

Questioner1 [Amy]: John's with the other group?
Ghost Box: Yes.

[*We switch over to Shawn and Dan, who has started a ghost box experiment downstairs.*]

Questioner3 [Dan]: Are you trapped here?
Ghost Box: Nope.

Questioner3 [Dan]: How many people are here like you?
Ghost Box: Fifty.
Ghost Box: Dead.
Ghost Box: Help.
Observer4 [Dan]: That is what we are here to do.

Questioner3 [Dan]: Do you need help?
Ghost Box: Water.
Ghost Box: Desperate.
Ghost Box: Need help.
Ghost Box: Help.
Ghost Box: Need your help.
Ghost Box: Yes, help!
Ghost Box: Dan.

Questioner3 [Dan]: Yes?
Ghost Box: Worship or get out.

Questioner3 [Dan]: Call on the name of Jesus.
Ghost Box: You found them.
Ghost Box: They are grounded.
Ghost Box: Exactly.

Questioner3 [Dan]: John, are you here?
Ghost Box [John]: I am.

Questioner3 [Dan]: What is your name?
Ghost Box: Tim.
Ghost Box: Someone needs help.
Ghost Box: Need help.

Questioner3 [Dan]: What do the others need?
Ghost Box: Stuck in here.
Ghost Box: No mistake.

Questioner3 [Dan]: Those who want to leave; all it takes is calling on the name of Jesus [*referring to Romans 10:13, "Everyone who calls on the name of the Lord will be saved"*].
Ghost Box: Angels are here!
Ghost Box [John]: Psalm 28. From scripture.
Ghost Box: Jesus help.

Okay, it is time to take a break and read Psalm 28 (NIV), [which John refers to].

1 To you, Lord, I call; you are my Rock, do not turn a deaf ear to me. For if you remain silent, I will be like those who go down to the pit.

2 Hear my cry for mercy as I call to you for help, as I lift up my hands toward your Most Holy Place.

3 Do not drag me away with the wicked, with those who do evil, who speak cordially with their neighbors but harbor malice in their hearts.

4 Repay them for their deeds and for their evil work; repay them for what their hands have done and bring back on them what they deserve.

5 Because they have no regard for the deeds of the Lord and

what his hands have done, he will tear them down and never build them up again.
6 Praise be to the Lord, for he has heard my cry for mercy.
7 The Lord is my strength and my shield; my heart trusts in him, and he helps me. My heart leaps for joy, and with my song I praise him.
8 The Lord is the strength of his people, a fortress of salvation for his anointed one.
9 Save your people and bless your inheritance; be their shepherd and carry them forever.

Questioner3 [Dan]: He is the only one who can.
Ghost Box: Here.
Ghost Box: Where do we find Him?

Questioner3 [Dan]: How many of you want to leave?
Ghost Box: How many.
Ghost Box: I said help.

Questioner3 [Dan]: How many of you are there?
Ghost Box: Thousand.
Ghost Box: Help.
Ghost Box: Christ help.
Ghost Box: Spirit.

Questioner3 [Dan]: John, are you helping here?
Ghost Box [John]: I'm wondering.

Questioner4 [Malachi, from SAI Next Gen]: Do you see a gate or a door?
Ghost Box: Of course.
Ghost Box: God opens it from his own.
Ghost Box: Listen.

Ghost Box: Here.

Questioner3 [Dan]: What are you trying to say?
Ghost Box: Impossible for me.
Ghost Box: Oh God, help.
Ghost Box: Please help.

Questioner3 [Dan]: Call out to him. He will help you.
Ghost Box [John]: The sacrifice, Jesus, has risen.
Ghost Box: What is happening?
Ghost Box: Tell us.

Questioner3 [Dan]: People can leave.
Ghost Box: Then take me there.

Questioner3 [Dan]: I can't but Jesus can.
Ghost Box: How?

Questioner3 [Dan]: Call on his name.
Ghost Box [John]: Nothing is impossible
Ghost Box: Save us, Jesus, please help.
Listener [Shawn]: WHOA [*hearing strange sounds in the box*].
Ghost Box: What happened to them?
Ghost Box: Priest?
Ghost Box: What just happened?
Ghost Box [Young child]: Left.
Ghost Box: We're not gone …
Ghost Box [Young child]: They departed.
Ghost Box: What happened?
Ghost Box: Come back here!

Questioner4 [Malachi]: Are you free?

Ghost Box: Lost.

Questioner3 [Dan]: Are people leaving?
Ghost Box: [*Sound of crying or wailing aloud*]
Ghost Box: Please help me.
Ghost Box: [*Crying*]: I can't do it
Ghost Box [John]: You must believe it.

Questioner3 [Dan]: All you have to do is call on the name of Jesus and believe. That's it.
Listener [Shawn]: A man just in and is, like, "Hey, I need help."
Ghost Box: Beautiful people left.
Ghost Box: I need help.
Ghost Box: I need help.
Listener [Shawn]: Everybody is, like, I need help, hey, I need help to, and me…
Observer5 [Malachi]: The gate is always open. All you need to do is believe.
Ghost Box: Lost.
Ghost Box: You found us.
Ghost Box: I need help.
Ghost Box: Listen.
Ghost Box: What happened to them?
Observer4 [Dan]: They left.
Ghost Box: Really?
Ghost Box: This is stupid.
Observer4 [Dan]: No, it's not stupid.
Ghost Box: No, it isn't.
Ghost Box: Object with you!
Ghost Box: Won't stop.
Listener [Shawn]: There is a guy who definitely does not believe.

I can clearly distinguish him from the others. He has the same voice every time. He is, like, he does not believe it.

Ghost Box [John]: Speaker.

Ghost Box [John]: I'm done.

Ghost Box: He's closing [the door or gate].

Ghost Box: [*Sound of a door closing*]

Listener [Shawn]: WOW, I just heard a door slam shut! Very loud.

Ghost Box: Asshole!

Ghost Box: [*Sound of someone knocking on a door*]

Ghost Box: He was there.

Ghost Box: What happened?

[*Dave calls down from the library and asks*, "Hey, guys, where are y'all at?]

Dan: We are in the ballroom.

Dave: Okay, cool, cuz I was hearing doors shut up here and I just didn't know if that was you moving around from room to room.

Dan: Reeeaaalllllyyyyy?

Listener [Shawn]: They are literally kinda talking to each other. You have one guy who was not believing or something and kinda laughing about everything. Trying to talk to this woman who was kinda like on the fence about everything. John just left, like literally closed the door and, like, said sorry.

Ghost Box: I can't understand it.

Ghost Box: Priest help.

Observer4 [Dan]: We have already told you what you have to do, and you are not believing. You are rejecting it [the message].

Ghost Box: Rejected!

Observer4 [Dan]: You are rejecting [*meaning "You are not rejected"*]. You could have left [with the others]; you still can if you would believe. You just saw it right in front of you.

Ghost Box: He has left.

Observer4 [Dan]: I know.

Questioner3 [Dan]: Do you have a hard time believing?

Ghost Box: Left.

Ghost Box: Hear me, priest.

Ghost Box: Lost in here.

Listener [Shawn]: They are kinda spinning their wheels, man.

End experiment.

Dan: Dude.

Shawn: How was that? [*Hearing only half the conversation, Shawn has no idea.*]

Dan: Off the chain.

Shawn: Okay.

Malachi: It was.

Shawn: Ugh. He's thinking that he got rejected, but in reality he is rejecting himself.

Dan: It is some kind of mind-set that he is stuck in.

Shawn: There is one guy that I could clearly tell he was off in left field somewhere. There were these other people that seemed like they were on the fence. They got into an argument once

John left [with the believers]. I could clearly hear John basically saying, "Hey, I've said what I have had to say, I have taken some people with me who believe." It was weird, because you could hear the strange sounds, like the transition where they immediately became light. The others saw it and were, like, WHOA, and then they left. Then John had a long dissertation with them, and they did not get it, so he was, like, okay, you know, I'm out. So you hear a door literally creak as it slowly closes, then clicks/latches shut. Then they are coming up to the door, knocking on it, calling John names for leaving.

Dan: Now here is an interesting thing that you didn't know. I got a call on the walkie right after you talked about the door. Dave had asked if we were upstairs, and I said no, we are in the ballroom. He said well, that's weird because I'm hearing a door close.

Shawn: [*Jaw dropped and stunned*]

Pearis Theatre, Giles County, Virginia

SAI Investigative Team Briefing
Pearis Theatre Investigation

At the Pearis Theatre in Giles County, Virginia, the spirits were able to respond instantly with appropriate responses to questions. In some cases they were able to complete full sentences, which is very rare in most ghost box demonstrations. During this investigation we had Beverly Boehm, a local journalist, participate as a guest in order to experience firsthand how to perform a Double Blind Ghost Box experiment. Beverly published an article from the events in a local magazine, *Flavours*, in December 2012, entitled "'Ghosts of Christmas Past' Still Reside in Giles County."

SAI in Flavours Magazine Winter 2012

Listener [Shawn]: We are in the main theater now, and we've got Billy up on the stage and Malachi and Brandon up front. We have Dan over here to the right, and I'm here in the middle, and we are going to do a ghost box session starting now. [*Mark audio*]

Questioner1 [Dan]: Is there someone here who would like to speak with us tonight?
Ghost Box: We're here.
Ghost Box: Don't record.

Questioner1 [Dan]: Ha-ha-ha, Mr. Real, is that you?
Ghost Box: Yes.

Questioner1 [Dan]: We are not recording a movie.
Ghost Box: Right.
Ghost Box: And I don't like this.

Questioner1 [Dan]: Why are you still here?
Ghost Box: Want to ... let go.

Questioner1 [Dan]: Do you feel like you need to stay here and take care of your theater?
Ghost Box: Theater, yes, I do.
Ghost Box: Tired.

Questioner1 [Dan]: Do you need help?
Ghost Box: Can't do this.
Ghost Box: I'm miserable.

Questioner1 [Dan]: We are here to help you if you need help.
Ghost Box: In dream.
Ghost Box: What happened to this great place? Turn it back.

Questioner1 [Dan]: How many of you are here?
Ghost Box: I am in here, one.
Ghost Box: You want to take us?

Questioner1 [Dan]: No, but we know someone who will. We can help you.
Ghost Box: Careful.
Ghost Box: Damn you.
Ghost Box: Damn you!

Questioner1 [Dan]: We can lead you to someone who can take you away [from here] to a better place.
Ghost Box: Stop it!

Questioner1 [Dan]: Do you need help?
Ghost Box: You could ...
Ghost Box: But we are dead people.

141

Questioner1 [Dan]: Yes …
Ghost Box: Backwards here.

Questioner1 [Dan]: … you are dead people, but it is not the end.
Ghost Box: I killed her behind you.

Questioner1 [Dan]: Okay, but this is not the end.
Ghost Box: Home.

Questioner1 [Dan]: There is another way.
Ghost Box: I can't do it.
Ghost Box: Careful, stop him.

Questioner1 [Dan]: Stop who?
Ghost Box: Help.
Ghost Box: Together.
Ghost Box: You're a spirit.

Questioner1 [Dan]: You want help?
Ghost Box: Every second here is …
Ghost Box: Death!

Questioner1 [Dan]: Do you know who Jesus is?
Ghost Box: Priest.

Questioner1 [Dan]: Yes?
Ghost Box: Guardians resist us.
Ghost Box: They're dead.

Questioner1 [Dan]: Yes, they are dead.
Ghost Box: You're an angel.
Ghost Box: They're calling us up … out.

Questioner1 [Dan]: They can still choose, we have seen it before.
Ghost Box: With others?
Ghost Box: They're watching us.

Questioner1 [Dan]: Who are they?
Ghost Box: Now he knows!
Ghost Box: They knew about it.
Ghost Box: He's here!
Ghost Box: Priest!
Ghost Box: They sent you to us.

Questioner1 [Dan]: Yes, I have been sent. We have been sent here to help you. But they can still choose. Do they have the ability to choose?

[Motion sensor goes off.]

Questioner1 [Dan]: Do they have the ability …

[Motion sensor goes off.]

Questioner1 [Dan]: Do they have the ability to choose?
Ghost Box: Not very clear.
Ghost Box: Unknown.
Ghost Box: Very doubtful.

Questioner1 [Dan]: You still have free will.
Ghost Box: Prison.
Ghost Box: Out of body.

Questioner1 [Dan]: Yes, but it does not matter. If you would only believe [it]. Is that what you want?

Ghost Box: Absolutely!

Questioner1 [Dan]: Okay, all you have to do is believe that Jesus came, died; he died for you …
Ghost Box: [interrupts] Ummm?

Questioner1 [Dan]: All you have to do is call on his name.
Ghost Box: In earth?

Questioner1 [Dan]: Call on his name.
Ghost Box: We are lost, buddy, because, don't you know, there's doubts?

Questioner1 [Dan]: John, are you around?
Listener [Shawn]: Mark audio. How is it going?
Questioner1 [Dan]: It's crazy.
Listener [Shawn]: Crazy good or bad?
Questioner1 [Dan]: No, no, it's good.
Listener [Shawn]: Good keep going?
Questioner1 [Dan]: Yeah.
Listener [Shawn]: Okay.
Questioner1 [Dan]: We are right in the middle of it. You need to keep going!
Listener [Shawn]: Oh, okay, sorry.

Questioner1 [Dan]: Who is the leader here?
Ghost Box: Warden.
Ghost Box: Is God the truth?

Questioner1 [Dan]: Yes.
Ghost Box: Oh dear.
Ghost Box: That son of a …

Questioner1 [Dan]: Who is talking right now?
Ghost Box: Prison.
Ghost Box: Prison keeper.
Ghost Box: He is dead.
Ghost Box: I'm a prison guard.

Questioner1 [Dan]: Listen, these people still have a right to choose!
Ghost Box: Can't save us.

Questioner1 [Dan]: YES, we can.
Ghost Box: It's zero.

Questioner1 [Dan]: We can't but we know someone who can.
Ghost Box: No chance.

Questioner2 [Billy]: Why do you say that?
Ghost Box [Woman's voice]: Hardheaded.

Questioner1 [Dan]: Can someone tell me who the leader is?
Ghost Box: Evil.

Questioner1 [Dan]: What is his name?
Ghost Box: Careful, dangerous.
Ghost Box [Steven]: I am Steven, the seeker.

Questioner1 [Dan]: Hi, Steven.
Ghost Box: I see a believer.
Ghost Box [Steven]: I just don't.

Questioner1 [Dan]: Steven, do you want help?
Ghost Box [Steven]: Broken.
Ghost Box [Steven]: We're a home.

Questioner1 [Dan]: Jesus can fix you. Even now. Even if you do not have a body.
Ghost Box [Steven]: We are seven.
Ghost Box [Steven]: Evils.
Ghost Box [Steven]: Say it!

Questioner1 [Dan]: Do you want to leave?
Ghost Box [Steven]: Here, yes.

End experiment.

SAI determined that Steven was a demonic spirit that also when by the name Seven. We found out later through other investigations that Seven is oppressing human spirits at various locations throughout the region.

The Triangle Field, Gettysburg

SAI teams up with Patrick Burke, cofounder of the American Battlefield Ghost Hunters Society, and Mary Russell to investigate several locations at the Gettysburg battlefield in Pennsylvania. The focus of the investigations was to explore possible opportunities for spirits from the beyond to communicate their perspectives from the events in their lives through the double-blind ghost box methods.

Shawn Taylor and Mary Russell (Triple Blind Config.)
Billy Meadows (Double Blind Config.)

[Shawn kicks off the experiment by asking a base question to see if anything responds to inquiries.]

Listener [Shawn]: Is anyone from the 124th here?
Ghost Box: We're all here, yes.
Ghost Box: The other soldiers are dead.
Ghost Box: What's happening?

[From here Patrick begins to question spirits from the Civil War while Shawn cannot hear them.]

Questioner1 [Patrick]: [Asks Dan] So Shawn can't hear anything I'm saying?
Observer [Dan:] No, he cannot hear you.

Questioner1 [Patrick]: [Smiles] Say a funny joke about Shawn. *[Laughs]* We will have to get this on camera for posterity. *[Laughs]*
Observer [Dan]: We will be a little stunned during the review later. *[Laughs]*

Questioner1 [Patrick]: Okay. Boy. I'm back here with my friend; you want to let us know what it sounded like back in July 1863?

Ghost Box: You're so clever [*referring to Patrick's joke*].

Observer [Patrick]: [*Laughs*]

Ghost Box: Good man.

Observer [Patrick]: Yeah, we like to joke a little.

Ghost Box: I'll say.

Observer [Patrick]: [*Laughs*]

Observer [Dan]: [*Laughs*]

Questioner1 [Patrick]: So, uh, how about letting us hear what it sounded like when you were hunkered behind the wall, and you tried to take the batteries.

Ghost Box: Two of them.

Questioner1 [Patrick]: Capture a few guns?

Ghost Box: Two of them, with us.

Ghost Box: People from the left.

Questioner1 [Patrick]: 124th, did you get your colonel ... back? ... His body?

Ghost Box: He's here.

Questioner 1 [Patrick]: Did you have to charge back into this field to get the colonel's body back?

Ghost Box: Isaac.

Ghost Box: Isaac.

Ghost Box: Over here.

Ghost Box: Dead.

Questioner 1 [Patrick]: That was the name of the colonel.

Ghost Box: Come and get him.

Observer [Dan]: The colonel that you were mentioning ... his name was Isaac?

Observer [Patrick]: I think his first name was Isaac ... Vincent? Is what the name was. Col. Isaac Vincent. But what happened is the colonel fell down during the first run. He died on a boulder in the Triangle Field. And then the lieutenant colonel came in to get him, and the lieutenant colonel died when bringing the colonel back.

Questioner 1 [Patrick]: Can you tell Shawn ...
Ghost Box: Lieutenant.

Questioner 1 [Patrick]: ...where the lieutenant colonel's body was where he fell?
Ghost Box: We all people perished.
Ghost Box: Attention!

Questioner1 [Patrick]: Tell me if I'm pointing in the right direction.
Ghost Box: How?

Patrick: [Asks Dan] Can I take him [Shawn] and walk him [Dan]? ...Yeah, yeah.

Questioner 1 [Patrick]: You tell us when to stop, boys.
Ghost Box: He's there beneath you ...
Ghost Box: Somewhere out there ...
Ghost Box: I'm ready.
Ghost Box: Isaac ... He's in trouble.
Ghost Box: Oh my.
Ghost Box: He stumbled.
Ghost Box: Handsome ...
Ghost Box: He's the first person from Virginia ...

Ghost Box: Lots of them here.

Questioner 1 [Patrick]: Not Georgia?
Ghost Box: Close … Round Top.
Observer [Patrick]: That's behind us.

Questioner 1 [Patrick]: Are you with the Orange Blossom Boys?
Ghost Box: He's having trouble …
Ghost Box: Help us …
Ghost Box: One stood up.
Ghost Box: And "cole-moh"
Ghost Box: Killed him.
Ghost Box: Round Top.
Ghost Box: Spirit is leaving …
Ghost Box: Impossible back then to help.
Observer [Dan]: How far is Round Top from here?
Observer [Patrick]: [*Points to Round Top Mountain*] Right back there.
Ghost Box: Three-thousand-person operation.
Observer [Patrick]: That's right. Thirty-five hundred charged here.

End experiment.

This experiment demonstrated the ghost box was able to validate details about Civil War history in which the listener [Shawn] had no knowledge of.

Patrick Burke did some research for this clip. He stated, "The Isaac mentioned is Colonel Isaac Nicoll of the 124th NY Infantry, the 'Orange Blossom Boys'; he died in the Triangular Field during the July 2nd action."

Michael and the Red Legged Devils

The Fourteenth Regiment New York State Militia was a volunteer militia regiment from the city of Brooklyn, New York.

Their nickname, the Red Legged Devils, which referred to their trousers, came from "Stonewall" Jackson during the First Battle of Bull Run. As they charged up Henry House Hill again and again, he cried to his own men, "Hold on, boys! Here come those red legged devils again!"

On June 4, 1854, part of the regiment, led by Col. Jesse C. Smith, helped quell the "Angel Gabriel Riot," so called because it was caused by one Michael, an anti-Catholic street preacher who called himself "the Angel Gabriel." The Fourteenth assisted police in making arrests.

Supernatural Media and the Trent Hall Media Group, in association with the American Battlefield Ghost Hunters Society, conducted three ghost box sessions at a location in Gettysburg that produced information referencing the Red Legged Devils and Michael. This is a significant clip, showing how deceived souls were freed from the lies of Michael and taken home to rest.

Note that there are several spirits talking throughout this transcript. They are Michael, the false prophet preacher, and/or his sons; a demon named Bezel; the men from the Fourteenth Regiment New York State Militia (Red Legged Devils)[1]; the townspeople deceived by Michael; and John, the High Priest who set them free.

Those Red Devils they ride, fighting off...

Shawn Taylor (Listener)
Gettysburg Investigation

[*While setting up the ghost box in the double-blind configuration*]
Listener [Shawn]: That's weird; it said "red devil," and it said it three times. That was strange. Hold on. Something is wrong.
Ghost Box: Devil, have you seen Rachael?
Ghost Box: In here, ride!
Ghost Box: Red devil, in us dead.
Ghost Box: Red devil, in here calling.
Ghost Box: As in, red leader sent me.
Ghost Box: Red devil in me, have you seen Rachael?
Ghost Box: In here rides, with us.
Ghost Box: A pound of flesh, dead!
Listener [Shawn]: Oh my God. Okay, that was really weird, because when I first turned the box on, it was just repeating itself over and over, with minor variations. I have never heard that happen before. Strange.

[*Note that this was not a device malfunction. Dave, a lead investigator with SAI, was conducting a ghost box experiment of his own and got similar rambling about the red devils.*]

Begin experiment.

Questioner1 [Dan]: We might be able to help you if you are willing to communicate.

Questioner1 [Dan]: Can you hear us?
Ghost Box: Infamous.

Questioner1 [Dan]: Are you infamous?
Ghost Box: Can't free us Priest'ah.
Observer1 [Dan]: We might surprise you.
Ghost Box: Impossible to take us.
Ghost Box: Bullshit.

Questioner1 [Dan]: Can you tell us who you are?
Ghost Box: Bezel [*Sound of a raven or crow heard through the box*]
Ghost Box: Get out of here.
Ghost Box: The virgin is in you.

Questioner1 [Dan]: Can you tell us who you are with?
Ghost Box: Pastor's son.

Questioner1 [Dan]: What pastor? Who is your father?
Ghost Box: Michael.
Ghost Box: Seventh son.
Ghost Box: Maybe three.

Questioner1 [Dan]: We are with a group of people that try to help people like you. Can you understand that?

Ghost Box: [*No response*]

Questioner2 [Mary]: We want to know your story. Tell us your story. Who are you?
Ghost Box: Going, and north.
Ghost Box: Shooting.
Ghost Box: Now the situation.
Ghost Box: With a hundred people or so.
Ghost Box: I counted myself.
Ghost Box: My ashes.
Ghost Box: In the wind.

Questioner1 [Dan]: Were you burned?
Ghost Box: I.
Ghost Box: Pack up your dog.
Ghost Box: Too late to die, infantry.
Ghost Box: Ace.
Ghost Box: Out.
Ghost Box: If you're lucky.
Ghost Box: Open it.
Ghost Box: Hard to play Michael.
Ghost Box: Because I couldn't fear the people.
Ghost Box: Obviously!
Ghost Box: Leaving us to die.
Ghost Box: All of us backed up.
Ghost Box: Eight brothers called. The people forsake you, any science.
Ghost Box: As in pull out the giant.
Ghost Box: Enough evidence.
Ghost Box: Know them all from here to preach.
Ghost Box: Who's afraid now?
[*Patrick comes up to Dan to see what is going on*]

Observer1 [Dan]: Mary asked the spirit to tell us its story, and it just went nuts.

Ghost Box: Joined by one per Captain.

Observer1 [Dan]: It's telling us all these details.

Listener [Shawn]: They are saying a lot of stuff that I'm missing.

Observer2 [Patrick]: Mary, is it multiple or just one?

Ghost Box: Let's turn around.

Observer3 [Mary]: Multiple.

Ghost Box: He went backwards.

Observer2 [Patrick]: Have we got a Mike or a John yet?

Ghost Box: Watch yourself.

Observer1 [Dan]: Yeah, we got Michael.

Ghost Box: Five men.

Ghost Box: That's it.

Ghost Box: Positive.

Ghost Box: Keep pointing.

[Note: Patrick was pointing to various locations, looking for the place where one of the spirits had passed.]

Ghost Box: Right there.

Observer2 [Patrick]: Right where I'm pointing. Okay.

Ghost Box: Red riders come.

Ghost Box: They're needed.

Ghost Box: Cool name, isn't it?

Questioner1 [Dan]: Who are the red riders?

Ghost Box: Those Red Devils they ride, fighting off …

Ghost Box: I'll fucking murder him!

Ghost Box: George!

Observer3 [Mary]: Patrick.

Questioner1 [Dan]: Who is George?

Ghost Box: Said Patrick, come back.

Ghost Box: Friend selfish.

Observer1 [Dan]: Mary, now that was important. He did not know we were calling Patrick over here.

Observer3 [Mary]: Yeah, not just that.

Ghost Box: Was real, though.

Questioner1 [Dan]: Who just touched my chest?

Ghost Box: He did.

Questioner1 [Dan]: Were you trying to intimidate me?

Ghost Box: Yes, he is.

Questioner1 [Dan]: Who are we speaking with now?

Ghost Box: The source.

Ghost Box [Female voice]: Hello?

Ghost Box [Female voice]: Who's here?

Observer3 [Mary]: Mary.

Ghost Box [Female voice]: I see, yeah.

Questioner1 [Dan]: Are you done?

Ghost Box: Going to heaven.

Ghost Box: Come inside and visit me.

Ghost Box: Your house.

Ghost Box: No pun.

Questioner2 [Mary]: Who are you going to visit? Who is inside?

Ghost Box: [Sound of singing]

Ghost Box: Moving up.

Questioner2 [Mary]: You can go inside, there's home.

Ghost Box [Strong male voice]: I call forth lions!

Questioner2 [Mary]: You can go home.
Ghost Box: Confederates.
Ghost Box: Who is like them?
Ghost Box: They're top spirit.
Ghost Box: This is defense.
Ghost Box: Go home.

Questioner1 [Dan]: What is his name?
Ghost Box: We're dancing.
Ghost Box: Holy Spirit.
Ghost Box: He's God.
Ghost Box: He found us, free.

[John intervenes and begins speaking to the spirits deceived by Michael's lies.]

Ghost Box [John]: Be careful.
Ghost Box [John]: This is the sixteenth revelation to the witness of Christ.
Ghost Box [John]: I am John; I say don't fall for this. I'll speak this simple warning.
Ghost Box [John]: Michael isn't a prophet of God.
Ghost Box [John]: He looks, afraid. He's the devil in you. A host to him.
Ghost Box [John]: The spirits of the dead.
Ghost Box [John]: It's not too hard to join us.

Questioner1 [Dan]: Is there a door?
Ghost Box: Go to him!

Questioner2 [Mary]: Make your way.
Ghost Box: What's happening? [*A strange sound is heard through the box, like a tractor beam in science fiction movies.*]

157

Listener [Shawn]: I heard a strange sound, like something goes *ZZZZOOOOPPP* away. Almost like an alien beam.

Questioner2 [Mary]: Make your way. That's right.
Ghost Box [John]: Come up, friend!
Ghost Box [John]: From now on this is your place.
Ghost Box [John]: For any of them who need help.
Ghost Box [John]: Worship.
Ghost Box [Angelic choir]: Come.
Ghost Box [Deep male voice but not John]: Good.
Ghost Box [John]: Here's a banquet.

Questioner1 [Dan]: Is there anything else to be said?
Ghost Box [John]: Look, there is appointed …
Ghost Box [John]: Computed for us to …
Ghost Box [John]: Possible for us to …
Ghost Box [John]: Set those free.

Listener [Shawn]: Mark audio. Umm, that was intense.

End experiment.

Heaven Underneath Our Feet

*The SAI Team Investigates the Triangle Field, Gettysburg
Triple Blind Ghost Box Experiment*

Ghost Box: Impact! Waves are coming in.
Ghost Box: Confederate. It's frightening.

Questioner1 [Patrick]: Is the Third Arkansas here?
Ghost Box: Yes, sir.

Questioner1 [Patrick]: Are you with the 124th New York? How about the 99th Pennsylvania?
Ghost Box: Last call. "Brass Cough" Infantry … place … weapon count. John passed out.
Ghost Box: I was twenty when it happened then.
Ghost Box: Follow big … (unknown word) … with us.
Listener2 [Mary]: I'm hearing booms and bangs.
Listener1 [Shawn]: Lots of … yeah … it does … it sounds like … just listen …
[Shawn hands the headphones to Patrick.] It sounds like a

bunch of guns going off. People are trying to talk, and boom boom. It's like you're right in the middle of the battle.

Questioner1 [Patrick]: There is still a lot of booming going on. It sounds like someone got shot.

Ghost Box: I'm shot.

Ghost Box: Are you David Trent?

Observer1 [Shawn]: Hey. I get to listen to this for a change.

Ghost Box: Winchester.

Listener3 [Patrick]: Boom, boom, boom, boom.

Questioner1 [Patrick]: This is Patrick and Mary. Do you want to give us a nice string of answers here?

Ghost Box: Show me.

Ghost Box: Country.

Questioner1 [Patrick]: This is damn hard!

Ghost Box: I was with America first.

Ghost Box: Colonel David, Pat Burke.

Questioner1 [Patrick]: Oh. Did you hear that? [*Asking another listener*] Oh, she can't hear me.

Ghost Box: Remember we all have this … once traveled.

Ghost Box: Died.

[*At this point Shawn resumes listening. He asks that we try to get the spirits to focus on the now instead of what happened when they died.*]

Ghost Box: Patrick.

Ghost Box: Available now.

Ghost Box: David was a father.

Ghost Box: These Yankees are dead.

Ghost Box: Four, three …

Ghost Box: There is one.

Questioner1 [Patrick]: Could you, uh … could one of you gentlemen step out? All we want to do is capture a bit of your life story. So we would like to know your name …
Ghost Box: You see it.

Questioner1 [Patrick]: Your wife's name …
Ghost Box: Isabella *"or Elizabeth"* …

Questioner1 [Patrick]: Or where you are from …
Ghost Box: Fort Donelson.

Questioner1 [Patrick]: I want you to step out from the conflict …
Ghost Box: Hunting.
Ghost Box: On foot.
Ghost Box: First time.

Questioner1 [Patrick]: Is this your first action?
Ghost Box: Seven. … We've been moved by twelve people with lantern light … waiting for survivors.
Ghost Box: Clergy.

Questioner1 [Patrick]: Do you need last rites?
Ghost Box: You're asking me?

Questioner1 [Patrick]: Yes.
Listener1 [Shawn]: Now, there were two people who responded to that. There was a lady that says, "Are you talking to me?" and a guy said something.
Ghost Box: Spirit.
Ghost Box: I'm frightened.

Questioner1 [Patrick]: Have you received your last rites?

Ghost Box: I'm listening … YES OR NO!
Listener1 [Shawn]: Okay. Something's changing.
Ghost Box: The iron door is open.
Ghost Box: Please come *[or "he said come"] [or "Jesus said come"]*
Ghost Box: What's happening?
Ghost Box: Your spirit isn't free.
Ghost Box: Okay. Then let's hear them!
Ghost Box: High, High Priest come!
Ghost Box: It's impossible.
Ghost Box: I won't leave.

Questioner1 [Patrick]: Are you waiting for someone? Who are you waiting for?
Ghost Box: My family.
Observer2 [Dan]: They're already gone.

Questioner1 [Patrick]: They have already moved on. Do you want to join them?
Ghost Box: Don't … stop.
Observer1 [Patrick]: I wonder if they understand that term? That's a modern term. So do you think we should say going into the grace of God or …
Observer2 [Dan]: Maybe. … "Going to heaven" is more universal.
Ghost Box: Seven hundred.

Questioner1 [Patrick]: Do you want to go to heaven now?
Ghost Box: Show us.
Ghost Box: The better truth.

Questioner1 [Patrick]: There is no judgment. You were following orders.

Ghost Box: Pardons.
Ghost Box: Holiness.
Ghost Box: Holiness.
Ghost Box: We are here and have the word.
Ghost Box: Come and worship.

[*At this point something happens that has not happened before during a session. Both listeners hear incredible music, which is overriding every channel on the radio. Both listeners excitedly hear it, but when the recording was reviewed the music was not there.*]

Listener1 [Shawn]: Holy cow! There is somebody singing! Somebody from heaven is singing! Praise Him! It is completely going through this whole thing!
Listener2 [Mary]: It's underneath!
Ghost Box: Come while there is time!
Listener1 [Shawn]: Somebody is saying ... I can't believe it.
Ghost Box: Devil work.
Ghost Box: And I saw a man ...
Questioner 1 [Patrick]: It's not the Devil's work...
Listener1 [Shawn]: I have never in my life heard anything like that. Oh my God, that was so cool. I cannot wait until you guys hear this! I mean you hear the radio flipping through like it normally does, but the whole time an angelic host is just singing its heart out all the way through. It's absolutely impossible, just singing alone across the sweeping! There's other people praising, not a part of the song, but like bystanders going, "Praise!" I mean, holy moly! That is probably the most incredible thing I have ever heard!

Contact the Authors

The Double-Blind Ghost Box website
http://TheDoubleBlindGhostBox.com

Contact Shawn Taylor
Shawn.Taylor@SupernaturalAI.com

Contact Daniel Morgan
Dan.Morgan@SupernaturalAI.com

The Double-Blind Ghost Box **on Facebook**
http://www.facebook.com/TheDoubleBlindGhostBox

Supernatural Anomaly Investigations (SAI) official website
http://www.SupernaturalAI.com
http://www.Supernatural-Media.com

SAI Email
Investigations@SupernaturalAI.com

SAI on Facebook
http://www.facebook.com/groups/113154475387350

SAI on YouTube
http://www.YouTube.com/user/SupernaturalMedia

Glossary

Double blind

1. Of or pertaining to an experiment or clinical trial in which neither the subjects nor the researchers know which subjects are receiving the active medication, treatment, etc., and which are not: a technique for eliminating subjective bias from the test results.

2. Of or relating to an experiment to discover reactions to certain commodities, drugs, etc., in which neither the experimenters nor the subjects know the particulars of the test items during the experiments

Electromagnetic field: A field of force associated with a moving electric charge equivalent to an electric field and a magnetic field at right angles to each other and to the direction of propagation.

Scientific method: The scientific method is the process by which scientists, collectively and over time, endeavor to construct an accurate (that is, reliable, consistent and nonarbitrary) representation of the world. Recognizing that personal and cultural beliefs influence both our perceptions and our interpretations of natural phenomena, we aim through the use of standard procedures and criteria to minimize those influences when developing a theory. As a famous scientist once said, "Smart people (like smart lawyers) can come up with very good explanations for mistaken points of view." In summary, the scientific method attempts to minimize the influence of bias or prejudice in the experimenter when testing a hypothesis or a theory.

Residual hauntings / residual phenomena: In the terminology of ghost hunting, residual hauntings, are repeated playbacks of auditory, visual, olfactory, and other sensory phenomena that are attributed to a traumatic event, life-altering event, or a routine event of a person or place, like an echo or a replay of a videotape of past events. Ghost hunters and related paranormal television programs say that a residual haunting, unlike an intelligent haunting, does not directly involve a spiritual entity aware of the living world and interacting with or responding to it.

Solipsism

1. The theory that only the self exists, or can be proved to exist.
2. Extreme preoccupation with and indulgence of one's feelings, desires, etc.; egoistic self-absorption.
3. The extreme form of skepticism that denies the possibility of any knowledge other than of one's own existence.

Endnotes

Chapter One

1. The scientific method is the process by which scientists, collectively and over time, endeavor to construct an accurate (that is, reliable, consistent, and nonarbitrary) representation of the world. See *University of Rochester, Department of Physics and Astronomy*, Home page of Prof. Frank L. H. Wolfs, Phy Labs, "Appendix E: Introduction to the Scientific Method," http://teacher.nsrl.rochester.edu/phy_labs/appendixe/appendixe.html.

2. Our videos can be viewed at http://SupernaturalAI.com/RAW and http://www.youtube.com/user/SupernaturalMedia.

3. Colonel Isaac Nicoll of the 124th New York Infantry was killed when his infantry unit defended against a Confederate assault on the Union left flank near Devil's Den on the second day of battle. *Gettysburg,* "Gettysburg Museum Exhibits," http://www.gettysburgfoundation.org/11.

Chapter Two

1. American photographer Attila von Szalay was among the first

to successfully record voices of the dead as a way to augment his investigations into photographing ghosts. He began his attempts in 1941, using a 78 rpm record, but it wasn't until 1956, after switching to a reel-to-reel tape recorder, that he believed he was successful. See *Culture and Communication*, Dead Media Archive, http://cultureandcommunication.org/deadmedia/index.php/Electronic_Voice_Phenomena.

2. Austin C. Lescarboura. *"Edison's Views on Life and Death"* An Interview with the Famous Inventor Regarding His Attempt to Communicate with the Next World. Scientific American October 30, 1920 pg. 446

3. Nevertheless, purported descriptions of Edison's invention do exist, stating it consisted of a microphone installed in a wooden box along with a large, potassium permanganate–filled aluminum cone and crossed by an electrode. See Carlos G. Fernández, *Psicofonías y Psicoimágenes* (Madrid: Ed. América Ibérica SA, 2002).

4. Master T, "History of EVP, Spirit Voice, Ghost Box, and ITC Communication," *livescifi.tv*, http://livescifi.tv/2011/08/history-of-evp-spirit-voice-ghost-box-and-itc-communication.

5. "'Hi Daddy, I Love You'—Engineer 'Talks' to His Dead Teenage Daughter after Developing Paranormal Detection Devices," *Daily Mail*, April 24, 2012, http://www.dailymail.co.uk/news/article-2134547/Hi-Daddy-I-love--Engineer-talks-dead-teenage-daughter-developing-paranormal-detection-devices.html.

Chapter Five

1. D. R. Khashaba, "Subjectivism and Solipsism," *Philosophy Pathways* no. 37 (July 28, 2002), http://www.philosophypathways. com/newsletter/issue37.html.

Chapter Nine

1. "The Red Devils," *Wikipedia*, http: //en.wikipedia.org/ wiki/14th_Regiment_(New_York_State_Militia).

Bibliography

Brune, François. *The Dead Speak to Us.* N.p.: Philippe Lebaud, 1988.

Chisholm, Judith. "Electronic Voice Phenomena." *ForteanTimes,* May 2005. http://www.forteantimes.com/features/articles/130/electronic_voice_phenomena.html.

Collins English Dictionary, complete and unabridged 10th ed., *q.v.* "electromagnetic field." http://dictionary.reference.com/browse/Electromagnetic Field.

"Edison and the Ghost Machine: The Great Inventor's Quest to Communicate with the Dead," http://paranormal.about.com/od/ghostaudiovideo/a/edison-ghost-machine.htm.

"Electronic Voice Phenomena: Atilla Von Szalay." *Culture and Communication*, Dead Media Archive. http://cultureandcommunication.org/deadmedia/index.php/Electronic_Voice_Phenomena.

Fernández, Carlos G. *Psicofonías y Psicoimágenes.* Madrid: Ed. América Ibérica, SA, 2002.

French, Chris. "Scientists Put Psychic's Paranormal Claims to the Test." *Guardian,* May 12, 2009. http://www.guardian.co.uk/science/2009/may/12/psychic-claims-james-randi-paranormal.

"Gary Galka: From Electrical Engineer to Ghost-Hunter," *Wizzley.* http://wizzley.com/gary-galka-from-engineer-to-ghost-hunter.

"Gettysburg Museum Exhibits." *Gettysburg.* http://www.gettysburgfoundation.org/11.

Austin C. Lescarboura. *"Edison's Views on Life and Death"* An Interview with the Famous Inventor Regarding His Attempt to Communicate with the Next World. Scientific American October 30, 1920 pg. 446

"'Hi Daddy, I Love You'—Engineer 'Talks' to His Dead Teenage Daughter after Developing Paranormal Detection Devices." *Daily Mail,* April 24, 2012. http://www.dailymail.co.uk/news/article-2134547/Hi-Daddy-I-love--Engineer-talks-dead-teenage-daughter-developing-paranormal-detection-devices.html.

Khashaba, D http://www.philosophypathways.com/newsletter/issue37.html. R. "Subjectivism and Solipsism." *Philosophy Pathways,* no. 37, July 28, 2002.

Master T. "History of EVP, Spirit Voice, Ghost Box, and ITC Communication." *livescifi.tv.* http://livescifi.tv/2011/08/history-of-evp-spirit-voice-ghost-box-and-itc-communication.

"New P-SB7 ITC Research Device." *Professional Measurement.* http://www.pro-measure.com/P_SB7_SB7_Spirit_Box_s/98.htm.

Paranormal-Encyclopedia.com, q.v. "Edison, Thomas." http://www.paranormal-encyclopedia.com/e/thomas-edison.

Posada, Janice. "Saying He Has Felt His Dead Daughter's Presence, an Engineer Develops Devices to Measure It."

Hartford Courant, April 23, 2012. http://articles.courant. com/2012-04-23/news/hc--melissa-galka-accident-paranormal-20120423_1_devices-paranormal-phenomena-electrical-engineer.

"The Red Devils." *Wikipedia*. http://en.wikipedia.org/wiki/14th_Regiment_(New_York_State_Militia).

Senkowski, Ernst. "Analysis of Anomalous Audio and Video Recordings." Presentation to the Society for Scientific Exploration, June 1995.

Shermer, Michael. *Why People Believe Weird Things: Pseudoscience, Superstition, and Other Confusions of Our Time.* New York: Holt Paperbacks, 2002.

"Who Invented EVP?" *Paranormalistics*, blog entry August 9, 2012, 3:10 p.m. http://paranormalistics.blogspot. com/2012/08/who-invented-evp.html.

Woolworth, Tim. "Ghost Boxes: Dedicated Ghost Boxes and Hacked Radio Ghost Boxes." *ITC Voices ... Talking to the Other Side*. February 26, 2011. http://itcvoices.org/ghost-boxes.

Matthew Moncrieff Pattison Muir. *"Residual Phenomena"* Popular Science Monthly. Volume 15. May, 1879

"Residual Hauntings / Residual Phenomena" Ghost Lab Glossary of Terms. http://dsc.discovery.com/tv/ghost-lab/about/glossary-of-terms.html

Index